Are you a frustrated environmental visions grind of program mar feel to you like more of for your program? Let L ... .ets help you!

As Bob Horton says, "There isn't much about leading for sustainable outcomes that I've not done wrong. Fortunately, good people over the years have helped me. **Lessons** is my way of sharing their wisdom along with what I've learned along the way."

In this sound bite driven world, leaders of workshops and new approaches are all too often forced to present only overviews of their subjects. This leaves out the fundamentals of creating the building blocks that keep their concepts stable under the pressures of daily implementation. What can get lost are the very details that help change agents make their concepts doable, day by day. **Lessons from the Streets** helps to fill in these blanks!

Lessons' format is simple and arranged in easily read chapters. If an affiliate director and/or board member would read, digest, and apply this accumulated wisdom and experience, their organization and community would benefit greatly. Extensive relevant background information provides complete and supplement the understanding of the answers. **Lessons** is a field manual for success for the professional-level program manager who really desires, and works to achieve, individual and community behavioral changes for quality of life improvement. I would like to provide each of our affiliates with a copy of **Lessons**!

—Robert Phelps, Executive Director of Keep Arkansas Beautiful and past Keep America Beautiful Board Member

More Kudos for Lessons from the Streets

YES! I am thrilled to see tried and true field experience brought to the fingertips of industry professionals. **Lessons** is more than a step by step of "How To" become a better affiliate. It gets to the grit of some of those hard to ask, and even unknown questions, and rewards its reader with higher-level thought processes and answers in a simplified format. The often seemingly daunting task of building more sustainable communities has now had a bright green light cast upon it. Our change-managing future just got a whole lot brighter, thanks to the positive energy in **Lessons**. It is certain to become a treasured resource for new and seasoned professionals alike, as they seek to persevere in their environmental leadership.—*Amy D. Reed, Executive Director, Keep Katy Beautiful, Board Member, Keep Texas Beautiful*

Lessons truly does hold a great deal of wisdom, coupled with practical knowledge. It is brimming with well-worded, straightforward information, the kind I counted on its author to deliver. It is sure to become a valued guidebook for KAB affiliates and other environmental program leaders in communities across America. As we persist month after month in attempting the seemingly impossible with so few resources, **Lessons** brings hope and added do-ability to our efforts. Thank you, Bob Horton, for taking the time to write this extra-green book!—*Donna Kliewer, Waste Services Manager, City of Allen, Texas and Keep Allen Beautiful Executive Director*

Wow, finally, a book that addresses the both the "why" and the "how" questions...and answers them! I did not know that I had 30 questions about strengthening our affiliate! However, chapter after chapter, **Lessons** has provided me with useful, practical strategies that will brighten our future and improve our behavior management capacity. The City of Covington will become cleaner, better at recycling and greener, thanks to **Lessons!** Where can I reserve my copy of the sequel? ;-)—*Sheila Fields, Solid Waste and Recycling Coordinator, City of Covington, Kentucky and Keep Covington Beautiful Board Member*

I liked the timing and flow of **Lessons** as it moves from one chapter to another. It delivers on various levels from simple, easy ideas to get one's attention up to higher levels of critical thinking about the "whys" that lie behind each question and response. **Lessons** is impressive and affordable. It will be a great teaching and training tool.—*Rick Hose, Keep Irving Beautiful Coordinator, City of Irving (Texas) Code Enforcement Department*

Lessons' style and content are equally impressive. It plainly reflects the common sense of someone with extensive experience in the field, successfully practicing community behavior management. One example of its pragmatic teaching would include "Give NO presentation without asking for a commitment to greater engagement." Right! Another is to treat our communities as a collection of sub-areas or "super neighborhoods" where people do so much of their day-to-day living. The reading of **Lessons** bolsters and documents the wisdom of long-time coordinators and hastens learning for new coordinators. It is truly a pocket field guide! I definitely recommend buying this book, reading it and then doing what it says. Your community will be better for it!—*Tammy Chan, Special Projects Manager, City Manager's Office, City of Grand Prairie, Texas*

LESSONS FROM THE STREETS

Other publications and unpublished materials by Robert Horton

Non-Fiction

1. <u>Ad-Wrap</u>: A Community News Bags to Litter Bags Program

2. <u>Apartments Rock the Green, Too!</u>: Collaboration Program and Tools Packet

3. <u>Assessment of HIV/AIDS Support Services and Challenges in Tarrant County, Texas, 1993-1994</u>

4. <u>Community Leadership Program for Neighborhoods, Curriculum Guide</u>

5. <u>Community Littering Field Report</u>

6. <u>Culture of Employee Wellness Promotion at Forty-Two, Tarrant County, Texas Workplaces, 1997-1998</u>

7. <u>Fir$T Things Fir$T</u>: Tuning Up Your Organization to Be Grant-Ready

8. <u>Green Corridor Thoroughfare/Interstate Targeted Litter Abatement Program</u>

9. <u>Green Dumpster</u>: A Business Waste Management, Measurement, and Education Program

10. <u>Green (Public) Events Guide</u>: A Simple Brochure

11. <u>Green Shopping Centers</u>: A Retail Waste Management Measurement and Education Program with Tools and Packet.

12. <u>Green Trucker</u>: A Transportation Waste Management Measurement and Education Program

13. <u>High Cost of Doing Too Little Litter Prevention with Tools Packet</u>

14. <u>Implications of Life/Work Studies on World Social Order</u>, With Dr. Linda Driskill, Emerita Professor of English, Rice University at Houston

15. <u>KAB System/Allen/Lewin/Prochaska-DiClemente, Comparative Analysis</u>: KAB's Golden Provenance

16. <u>Keep America Volunteering White Paper and Tools Packet</u>

Fiction

Papers and publications listed above may be available by contacting the author, Bob Horton, at Sustainable Opportunities and Solutions via Facebook or by email at mailto:bob.horton@rshorton.com.

LESSONS FROM THE STREETS

ROBERT S. HORTON, M.S.

Lessons from the Streets

Copyright © 2015 Robert S. Horton

SUSTAINABLE OPPORTUNITIES AND SOLUTIONS, INC.
PUBLISHER

Editor, LaRee Bryant, Ruby Moon Press

Formatting and Cover Design by Anessa Books

Cover art by Benoit Charton

ISBN-13:9781522900252

Dedication

This field guide offer insights into learning, through the Keep American Beautiful System, to lead for change that lasts. It is dedicated to three people; all early adopters as well as innovators whose influence from the 1970s and 1980s still impacts the Keep America Beautiful System, KAB and the management of change for the better at the community level. They are William ("Poppa Bill") Nash, Barbara Lee Mason, and Marilyn O. Godwin Tipton. They were three of America's earliest and always most accomplished KAB System program proponents.

Bill, as Keep America Beautiful's Vice-President of Field Services working out of your Middle America office in Grand Prairie, you brought to your work an enduring commitment to the startup and continued success of entire community programs as they strove to become cleaner and greener on a sustained and sustainable footing that remains legendary. You ushered in over 400 KAB System affiliate programs. You showed them the unique "KAB Way," teaching them its powerful steps and then holding their hands until they could fly on their own, achieving and sustaining cleaner, greener, better communities.

Barbara, your patience and belief in the power of caring people was awesome! It was such a joy to watch you extend that caring to the groups, organizations, communities, and even whole states where those individuals lived, worked and played. Therein lay your highest genius and talent. You always focused on the enormous potential of "working through existing organizations," helping them excel and then letting them have all the credit!

Marilyn, you taught hundreds of us invaluable lessons in the fine old practice of Snookering for the Good with style, artistry, and panache. You also taught us that shame and timidity had no place in the relentless pursuit of the resources to create a cleaner, more beautiful world. And, you shared with Barbara a limitless belief in our beloved KAB System nee Clean Community System and its underlying Normative System Culture Change Process. Your greatest skill lay perhaps in your dedication to seeing goals plainly expressed and projects to meet those goals well-planned and well-executed. I never saw a project write-up of yours that I didn't want to steal and did! Your deft integration of the KAB System with adaptations from your Junior League project management experiences had people of all ages (and many countries) doing sophisticated behavioral change management with surprising ease.

Here's to you, Poppa Bill, Barbara, and Marilyn. Please forgive the errors and mental missteps that you find here. The fault for them is squarely on my shoulders. You are sorely missed and fondly remembered as dedicated professionals and my great friends. Wherever I go to work with others who are seeking better places in which to live, work and play, you go with me, quietly and unseen, my mentors and coaches still.

God bless you each and all, my friends. Rest in Peace.

No man is an island, entire of itself;

Every man is a piece of the continent, a part of the main.

If a clod be washed away by the sea,

Europe is the less as if a promontory were, as well as if a manor of thy friends or of thine own were.

Any man's death diminishes me,

because I am involved in mankind;

And therefore, never send to know for whom the bell tolls;

it tolls for thee.

Devotions, Meditation XVIII, John Donne, 1623

Table of Contents

Program Design and Execution Questions   97

Supplemental Questions   137

Lessons is available from Amazon in both hardcover and e-print formats. Supplemental full color PowerPoint and handout teaching and learning materials for *Lessons* are in process. To be notified by the author when they are ready, please email mailto:bob.horton@rshorton.com. **Your comments and questions are welcomed and absolutely solicited!**

Acknowledgements

It is my pleasure to acknowledge the following professionals of many fields who have enriched my understanding of human behavior or made time to improve this book in so many ways with constructive criticism edit it and by providing me with graphics. I could not have written and produced this book without the help of every one of them.

Dr. Morris Massey, Ph.D., Cindy Phillips, and Levi Williams introduced me to understanding of the major forces at work in our society to mold us all and our behavior. Mead D'Amore's summary reporting of General Electric's involvement in the first Malcolm Baldrige Excellence Awards gave me real insights into top-level management thinking and strategies. Drs. James O. Prochaska and Carlo DiClemente, Ph.D. brought to us a better understanding of the stages that people go through in deciding to change...or not. Michael Samuelson, M.A. described application of the stages of change theory to public health education.

Dr. Robert F. Allen, Ph.D., designer of the field-proven Normative System Change Process, created the Keep America Beautiful System for KAB affiliates. His son, Dr. Judd Allen, Ph.D., has become a friend and been a steady source of encouragement in the ultimate development of this book. William "Poppa Bill" Nash first, and persuasively, introduced me the Keep America Beautiful System. When I left his first presentation, I said to myself, "This is dynamite and not just for litter. I want to spend the rest of my life using this knowledge to help communities better make better decisions." And so I have. Marilyn O. Godwin of Pensacola/Escambia County and Barbara Mason of the Keep Georgia Beautiful office were friends, teachers and coach for me as I sought to put the KAB System to work in Houston which was, at the time, the largest application of the system ever.

Cecile Carson has also been a friend, a mentor, and a "clarifier" for me. Her experience with over 600 assorted Keep America Beautiful affiliates informs, enlightens, and brings added warmth to every conversation we have both professional and personal. It was she, in fact, who helped bring me back into the KAB field after alcoholism, even in recovery, had severed my strong connections. LaRee Bryant, friend of many years and accomplished author, has helped to guide my every step in writing and publishing my first book. It was she who led me to my cover design and formatting editor, Merry Bond.

My first two professional reviewers and commenters were Sheila Fields, activist par excellence and Solid Waste and Recycling Coordinator with the City of Covington, Kentucky, and Robert Phelps, State Leader and Executive Director of Keep Arkansas Beautiful. Together, they encouraged me, gave me pointers, and helped to make this a more useful resource.

Fran Burns, colleague and friend taught me almost daily about the realities of applying the KAB System to smaller communities. No one simplifies fund raising basics better than does Jean Block, guru extraordinaire. I became acquainted with Dr. Michael Beyerlein as a student in his doctoral courses at the University of North Texas on Organizational Dynamics. His research illuminated my grasp of the sobering rate of failures of professionally led culture change projects in the American workforce. And, finally, J. Howard Rambin III, my career benefactor, sine qua non friend, colleague, and co-conspirator since 1977. It was you who boiled our challenges at Keep Houston Beautiful down to two sentences: "Nobody is for litter, so the question is "how do we organize 1.3 million Houstonians?" Always there with your steel trap mind in the "On" position. You started this, recruited, and supported me, have always been there for me. There are not words to express my gratitude for your contributions and your continued friendship!

Foreword

Across the years, I've worked in the field as a KAB System affiliate program director, taught college and graduate level classes in volunteer management, and spent many hours leading workshops. Numerous questions have come up more than have others while responses have not found their way into workshops manuals...or have been buried in those same manuals.

This handbook is written in response to those questions and I hope you'll join me in viewing ***Lessons from the Streets*** as a conversation about them between the two of us. ***Lessons*** provides us with a series of opportunities for "virtual conversations" with one another. With each question addressed here, I get the honor of having you as the proverbial "fly on the wall." You are there as I endeavor to give a hypothetical colleague the best answers I can in a very short period of time...as if they were over lunch between workshops at a conference, for example. You get to try out the answers you like on your own schedule. If you try one and it does not work, please let me know. I'll try to include your experience in the next revision to ***Lessons***.

After each response is a teaching tool in the form of the copy for a PowerPoint slide or a document. The plan is to provide you with a visual reference as you are studying or referencing each lesson – and to help you provide a handout for your key volunteers such as board members. My goal is for you and your key volunteers to become more confident masters of the KAB System process!

It isn't feasible to include all the tools that follow the chapters in this handbook. But a set of full-color, full-sized digital copies can be downloaded for a small fee. Check out Sustainable Opportunities and Solutions on Facebook. I wish you good reading, good learning and a cleaner, greener community to live in...soon!

Introduction

I find that most American communities believe that "a cleaner community is a better community," but that many struggle physically and financially with making that happen for themselves on a sustainable and affordable basis.

If we visit these communities, we typically find that there is no lack of activity, of cleanup-spruce up-paint up activity, of annual events, of hands full of spirited citizens doing all they can to show community pride and of those willing to point out that litter is a real problem. Unfortunately, all this activity and interest often leads not to a smaller problem but the need for even more activity. The key is to transform active energy into more effective activity; to truly work smarter, not just harder.

Litter however, or more accurately littering, is a sneaky, powerful, often baffling and surprisingly expensive challenge. It is sneaky in part because it will not stay where it is generated so it can be cleaned up. It is powerful because, upon inspection, we find that it is happening in virtually every corner of our community. And it is baffling because it seems almost incomprehensible that others would simply throw down all the litter initially find around us.

This handbook is intended to reveal littering's secrets, to rob it of its power to overwhelm our resources, and to offer explanations of the littering phenomenon that lead us toward fighting it more effectively. ***Lessons*** is largely provided as a supplement, a field manual, for those who have completed at least their basic training with Keep America Beautiful. New coordinators of local affiliates and key volunteers with those affiliates need the overviews provided by such training. This especially applies as to the administration, event planning, and reporting aspects of running a locally owned and operated KAB affiliate in good standing, which is a prerequisite for making the most of this book!

Lessons comes to you as a handbook so that it can be readily taken in a bit at a time, often to help answer a single specific question that has arisen about changing the habits of large numbers of local citizens. *Please write in this handbook*!

It also hopes to be a useful tool bag for non-KAB community leaders, whether elected, corporate or volunteer, who wish to bring about lasting change that can stand the test of time.

Much has been written about leadership, especially since the World War II years when an understanding of leadership – how to identify it, measure it, and teach it – was considered to be a key to winning that war. The overwhelming majority of the literature and discussion in the intervening time has focused on leadership traits and leadership styles.

This handbook contends that lasting leadership is more situational; it is as much about the led as it is the leader. Leaders come and go, but the values and behaviors of whole groups evolve more slowly. They persist over amazing lengths of time; witness the male tie and ladies' skirts!

This handbook is about fostering lasting change in large groups and requires but one basic set of leadership traits, style and circumstances. It is about the traits of openness and inclusion.

Taken together, openness and inclusivity allow us to share *what* we have learned from with others, while listening carefully as those others share their thoughts on *how* best to accomplish those things in their community.

We must remember that none of knows it all and that all of us are always smarter than any one of us.

Basic Questions about Litter and Littering

Chapter 1
Why Do People Act as They Do?

Perhaps the most frequent question raised in the work of KABS professionals is: Why DO (How CAN) people litter anyway? Not having a working theory in response to this question and incorporating that understanding into our programs is one of our greatest barriers to bringing about sustained change.

The core contention of **Lessons** is that much of what people do is driven by their social environment. We all make dozens if not hundreds of decisions daily from what to wear and what to eat for breakfast in the morning to where to eat dinner and what time to go to bed. Yet, the majority of those decisions are made within a context, a system within which we must choose among choices already determined by the tens of thousands of decisions already made by the others who make up our culture. The color and types of shoes available to us and the kinds of homes, cars, watches and medical care we can afford are all largely molded not by us but by others. In addition, even as we seek to influence others using our finite affiliate resources, they are constantly being bombarded with thousands of highly influential messages a day from three levels of influence within the larger system that surrounds us all:

Macro Influencers
State and Federal Government, National Radio, TV, Print Press, Social Media, and the Internet

Mezzo Influencers
Churches/Faith Groups, College Peers, Local Government, Local Media, Neighbors, Schoolmates and Teachers, Special Interest Groups, and Workplace Peers

Micro Influencers
Family, Close Friends

Macro Influencers, including social media, are largely beyond our power to reach or relate to often. Even when we receive national media coverage or enjoy the benefits of a particular piece of new national legislation, those media and legislative influences will pass on to the next topic within days if not literally seconds. Littering is with us every moment while macro influencers are forever moving on. Further, the multiplicity of traditional and social media "channels," means that even the strongest of messaging is received by an increasingly splintered audience. This splintering lessens any on-going impact on our local audience.

Micro Influencers are also difficult for us to reach out to with much effect. It is not that we cannot call, mail or email our immediate circle of family members and friends. We can...often. However, in the average community, there is just one of us and a handful of core volunteers while there are tens of thousands of "them." There simply are not enough of us to reach out one-on-one to all of them, even if a single contact were capable of changing their behavior patterns immediately and forever.

This leaves us looking for dynamic partners, groups that we can actively work *through* to achieve our common goals.

Mezzo Influencers are the partners we need to recruit. The list provided here only begins to detail the kinds of already formed and active groups and organizations that we can work with and through. They are the potential "wholesalers" of our messages. For example, in Irving, Texas at the Keep Irving Beautiful program, there was one or two of us on staff and a small board of directors much of the time. That meant that fewer than 20 of "us" were tasked with effectively reaching out to over 200,000+ of "them." In our favor, there were "only" about 15,000 businesses, neighborhood associations, schools, churches, media outlets and government agencies. Still a daunting number and we had to set priorities. But, interfacing our team of key players in a pool of 15,000 organizations seemed much more doable.

Speaking of key organizations, it is well to identify what might be called "double leverage" players. Our Chamber of Commerce was a double leverage partner because working with them first allowed us to work with their high profile work group. Secondly, it allowed us to leverage that relationship and reach out with enhanced credibility to their 2,000 members. Beyond that, our documented experiences with the Chamber gave us a better "face" when we then reached out to the other 6,100 known businesses in town.

As we can see, one of the first action items that every affiliate can get busy doing is "listing." Working with our volunteers, we can develop lists of key groups in each of the segments noted above, identifying their leaders, meeting schedules, contact information, and written missions if possible. Our local newspapers in particular and Chamber of Commerce can often be especially useful in this regard. Our goal is to use these lists to help us get invited to make brief informational presentations about our programs and our goals. Our using these presentational opportunities to invite them to host full 2-hour to 4-hour onsite training session should be a top priority. At these brief presentations, we will also have the opportunity to "ask for the order," to ask them to support us in numerous ways. We can ask them:

- To provide a representative of their organization to our board or an appropriate committee.
- To ask us back for progress reports annually.
- To provide volunteers for various events or to meet specific needs such as designing a website, painting our offices, providing an appropriate meeting space for trainings, updating city ordinances, etc.
- To be open to supporting us financially.

The order we should most want to fill when we invest time and energy to make an introductory presentation is to get them to hold on-site workshops at their workplaces, learning places, etc. so they can begin the task of changing community culture where they have the greatest influence and the most to gain.

A good policy to adopt is to **Never Make An Informational Presentation or Briefing Without Asking for an Order in Writing!** This is true regardless of the ask, as noted above. Short presentations followed by applause may feel good but they are simply insufficient to bring about change for the better much less lasting change.

NOTES:

Why Do People Act As They Do?

Macro Influencers

State and Federal Governments,
National and Social Media,
The Internet

Mezzo Influencers

Churches/Faith Groups, Local Government, Local
Media, Neighbors, School and College Peers,
Special Interest Groups, and Workplace Peers

Micro Influencers

Family, Friends, Social Peers

Figure 1

Chapter 2
Isn't All Litter Caused by Individual Acts of Littering?

Actually littering happens in several ways and understanding these modes of litter generation can help us develop more effective programs and drive ordinance and policing language that does not penalize "the accidental litterer."

- **Accidental/Incidental** littering occurs when, for example, the wind snatches an individual napkin from our picnic table and blows it into the nearby lake or pond or when fast food wrappers inadvertently fly out of our car window when we absent-mindedly open it. Trying to totally prevent or prosecute such littering is likely to be a fruitless use of energy and resources.

- **Habitual** littering by an individual is a different matter. This is the repetitive failure to properly contain trash, to retrieve loose debris, and, of course, to willfully or thoughtlessly litter, such as throwing cigarette butts in the street. This kind of littering can and should be addressed.

- **Normative or "Normal"** littering is habitual littering done by many members of the community...a half, or even more. Broader, on-going programs to address this kind of widespread dysfunction are needed. When frequent, casual littering becomes accepted, expected, traditional, then its entire support system must be confronted.

- **Cultural** or Systemic and repeated littering occurs when habitual or normative littering are supported by:
  o archaic laws,
  o inadequate technology,
  o unclear consequences,
  o un-even or "hidden" enforcement and
  o ineffective education.

When the unwritten rule is that littering and failing to properly handle solid waste have become a part of the culture in our community, it is these five strategic influences that must be changed for the better.

NOTES:

Four Levels of Littering

1. Accidental/Incidental

2. Habitual

3. Normal/Normative

4. Cultural/Systemic

Figure 2

Chapter 3
Nobody Likes Litter, So Why Do People Think It's OK?

A range of attitudes from denial to indifference to discrimination help foster continued litter generating behavior and consequences. These attitudes must be addressed in our program structure and content. The attitudes that must be dealt with include:

- **Stoic Gatekeepers**: These are key players in public and private positions to govern how waste is handled (or recycled) and retrieved and/or to promote cleanliness...or slovenliness. All too often, gatekeepers resist change for the better, saying "I've always done it this way; why should I be the one to change?"

- **Accepter/Deniers**: These are those who look about them and "do not see litter" or do not view cleaning up the litter they see as a problem or as an economic development opportunity and decide that "things are good enough." Good enough in their eyes becomes the enemy of excellent.

- **Helpless Victims**: These hapless folks are all of us who experience the consequences of inaction by Gatekeepers and Accepter/Deniers. "What can *I* do? People will think I am crazy, even hurt me, if I say or do anything!" We also say, "I never litter!" But, read on as we may very well be unwittingly a part of the problem!

- **Blaming-Placing Witnesses**: Few of us are long comfortable as victims. So, we become blame-placing witness of litter and littering. We say "It's kids in fast cars, fat cats, and furriners...not us at fault!" It is we who turn to local government and demand that this or that law be passed, ordinance be enforced, trapped litter be cleaned up. In this, we lead local government to spend its slender resources on quick fixes when in fact a more sophisticated, long-term approach would be much better. Only when we fully and properly contain loose trash every time and keep our property and the property for which we are responsible free of trash -- including trash that may have blown from elsewhere – all the time, and we never purposely or accidentally litter, are we truly blameless?

- **Well-Rewarded Litterer**: Litterers are well-rewarded by a culture that fails to pass, teach about and enforce effective litter laws and even cleans up after him or her. Lacking enforced consequences, the litterer justifiably believes that "no one cares." It almost seems OK to litter where there is already litter and someone else will ultimately pick it up. "Besides," he or she may think, "I'm creating jobs!"

Finally, we must focus first on the attitudes and behaviors of our Gatekeepers. Their best practices lead others to change their behaviors toward a cleaner...or a dirtier...community. A bonus is that they are far fewer in number compared to the entire population. For example, in one affiliate with a population of about 200,000, the estimated number of workplaces was 8,100. And, 25% of those employers, many of them the largest in town, belonged to the Chamber of Commerce. Obviously, collaborating with the Chamber to engage their members first was an excellent way to begin reaching out to the other 6,100 workplaces in town.

Spending the time to develop working relationships with other key organizations is far more efficient and less stressful over time than forever going it alone.

NOTES:

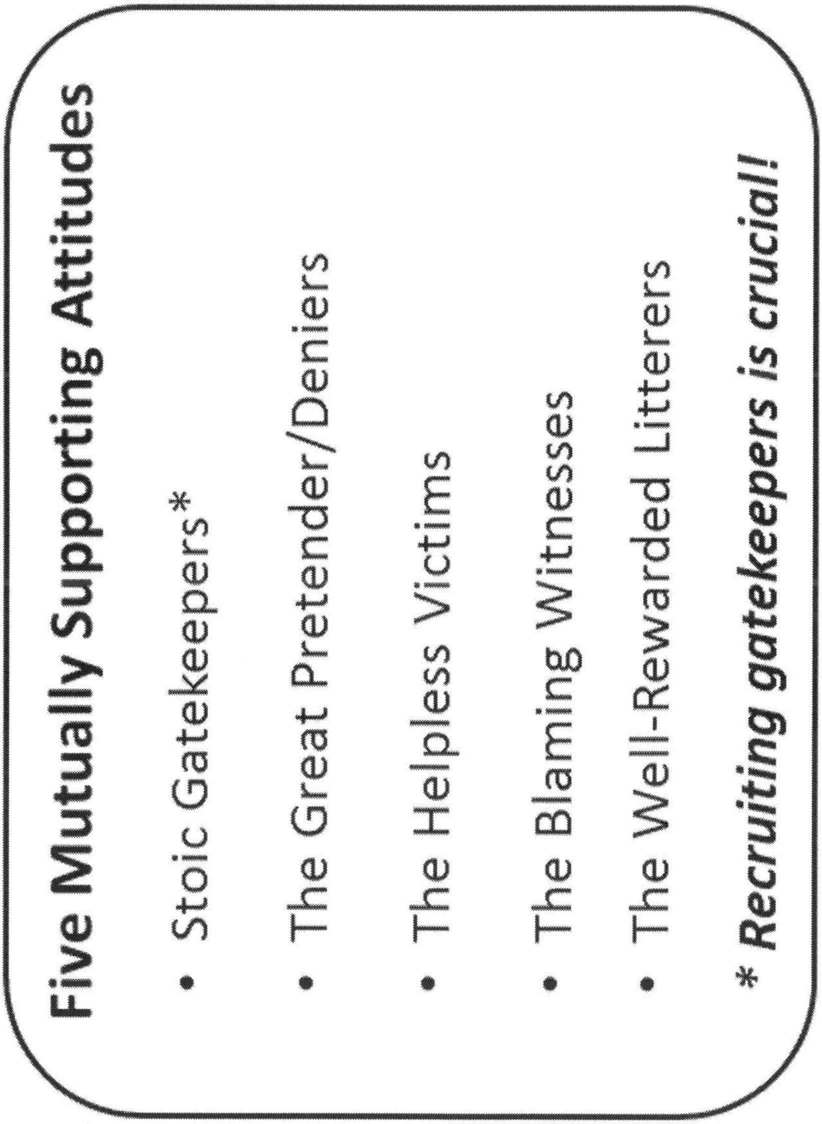

Five Mutually Supporting Attitudes

- Stoic Gatekeepers*

- The Great Pretender/Deniers

- The Helpless Victims

- The Blaming Witnesses

- The Well-Rewarded Litterers

Recruiting gatekeepers is crucial!

Figure 3

Chapter 4
Isn't Leading a Program for Lasting Change Just a Matter of Persistence?

Yes and no. Sorry about that!

Persistence can be powerful. American literature in particular often raises individual persistence to legendary status. President Calvin Coolidge wrote, "Nothing in the world can take the place of persistence. Press on!" He made a good point as far as it goes. This book began over 10 years ago!

However, persistence alone is often not enough for the persistent flapping of our arms will never let us begin to fly. Likewise, the experience of hundreds of American communities is that they clean up annually, monthly or weekly, but few of them can afford to clean up every time they become only slightly littered. This is because the underlying system of unwritten rules in the form of community norms that nurture litter production are more powerful than their persistently periodic cleanup efforts.

Norms in the form of unwritten rules are all around us. They lead us to whispering in church, to yelling at ball games, to speeding only a little bit when driving our automobiles and to sitting at the same place to eat our dinners at home at night. If you question the power of unwritten rules, sit in someone else's traditional place at the dinner table tonight, or park your car where they normally park or crawl into their side of the bed. Do all three and see what happens!

The fact is that fostering cultural changes, even relatively minor changes, is a sophisticated and complex challenge. It requires persistence and determination, but it also requires sophistication. Even then, as Dr. Michael Beyerlein, Professor of Organizational Dynamics at Texas A&M University, found in a 2002 study, roughly 70% of all corporate culture change initiatives do not meet their initials goals." Numerous more recent studies confirm this finding, he says.

Bringing that hard reality home is that the difficulty of trying to change littering and recycling behavior across entire communities has been compared to teaching an entire community to drive on the left side of the road instead of the right!

Simply put, "Just say No!" and "Just say Yes!" did not work addressing top U.S. health concerns such as smoking. Despite the best efforts of smoking cessation programs over a 50-plus year period, almost 20% of in American adults still smoke. In Texas the dedicated efforts of tens of thousands of individuals, organizations, communities, government and industry, have apparently yielded a recycling rate of only about 18% according to a recent statewide study by STAR, the State of Texas Alliance for Recycling.

Nonetheless, one elegant template for understanding the true scope of the challenges facing change planners is available. It was described by the Westinghouse Nuclear Fuels Division during the time that the former Mead D' Amore led WNFD to become one of the first ever recipients of the Malcolm Baldrige Award. Amended from its original purpose by this author to include the KAB System, it lays out many elements of a complex change management system on one page. As amended, it proposes that Vision + Skills + Incentives + Resources + Action Plans + Winning Strategies Yield Change for Good...Good That Lasts. This unified overview of large-scale behavior change management offers insightful corollaries:

- A Lack of Vision Yields Confusion
- A Lack of Skills Yields Anxiety
- A Lack of Incentives Yields Gradual Change
- A Lack of Resources Yields Frustration
- A Lack of Action Plans Yields False Starts
- A Lack of Winning Strategies Yields False Victories

This versatile tool is useful both prognosis (projection) and diagnosis (problem identification). For example:

- Prognosis: "This organization will benefit from its clear and motivating statement of vision that minimizes confusion at all levels.
- Diagnosis: "Marked levels of confusion in this organization or program, strongly suggest the need for a unifying vision that is shared by all of its members."

NOTES:

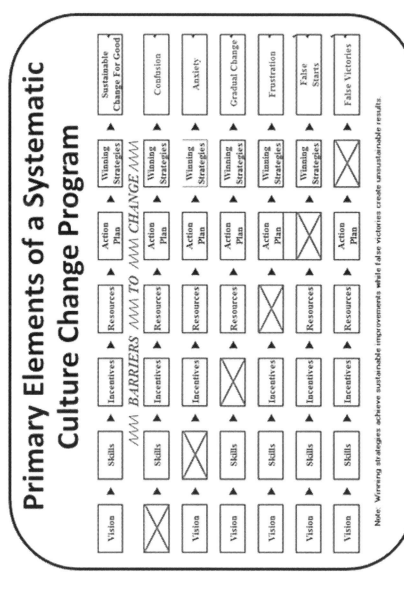

Figure 4

Chapter 5
What Is Our Greatest Hidden Challenge
Back Home?

Our greatest challenge when we are at any workshop, speech or conference presentation is that of overcoming our natural skepticism and naiveté so that we can recognize good ideas and gain glimpses of ways to employ those ideas back home.

Our greatest challenge when we get back home is to hold tight to those ideas while overcoming our volunteers' and boss' natural skepticism and naiveté.

Ironically for them, there is great comfort in what they already know... even if what they know is not working. This very human characteristic both limits and protects us. It is seen among abusive relationship victims, among newly released prisoners and soldiers...and sometimes among us KAB System professionals.

When we arrive back home from our first KAB National Conference, or our fifth or our tenth, we again rejoin our community of friends and colleagues who were not at the conference with us. As the founder of our KAB System taught us early on, their limited understanding of what needs doing to fight litter, to promote recycling and to support higher levels of beautification will tend to focus them on what they already know.

- Doing more clean ups, recycle ups and green ups; typically annual events.
- Sponsoring more projects such as parades, fairs, school appearances, etc.
- Recruiting more volunteers for our affiliate organization.
- Planning campaigns to "make more people aware of the litter problem.

They will cling to these things even though they have not solved the litter problem in the past. They will expect us, openly or unconsciously, to go along with them and not bother them with new ideas and initiatives. They will hew to what is known, what is comfortable. In addition, our own aversion to resistance, to drama, will draw us toward going along to get along.

Absolutely no one should expect us to sacrifice our jobs to make a point, but struggle we must. Who else is there to be aware of this pressure yet persist in order to bring about measurable change in spite of it? Hope though we might for someone else to take on this task, we are the ones that our community has been waiting for! Being change agents means that we will, to a greater degree than most, be somewhat alone, in front of the pack, in the lead, not following. Ours is the riskier path but, if we are to spark change, we must get better at being the change we want to see happen, at walking the path that we want others to take, not just talking about it.

So, our greatest challenge when we get back home is not that of being a part of bringing about change, but that of giving in to our own to take the easier, softer way, and avoid the drama of bringing about radical change for the better.

> *"To accomplish great things, we must not only act,*
> *but also dream; not only plan, but also believe."*
>
> *Anatole France"*

NOTES:

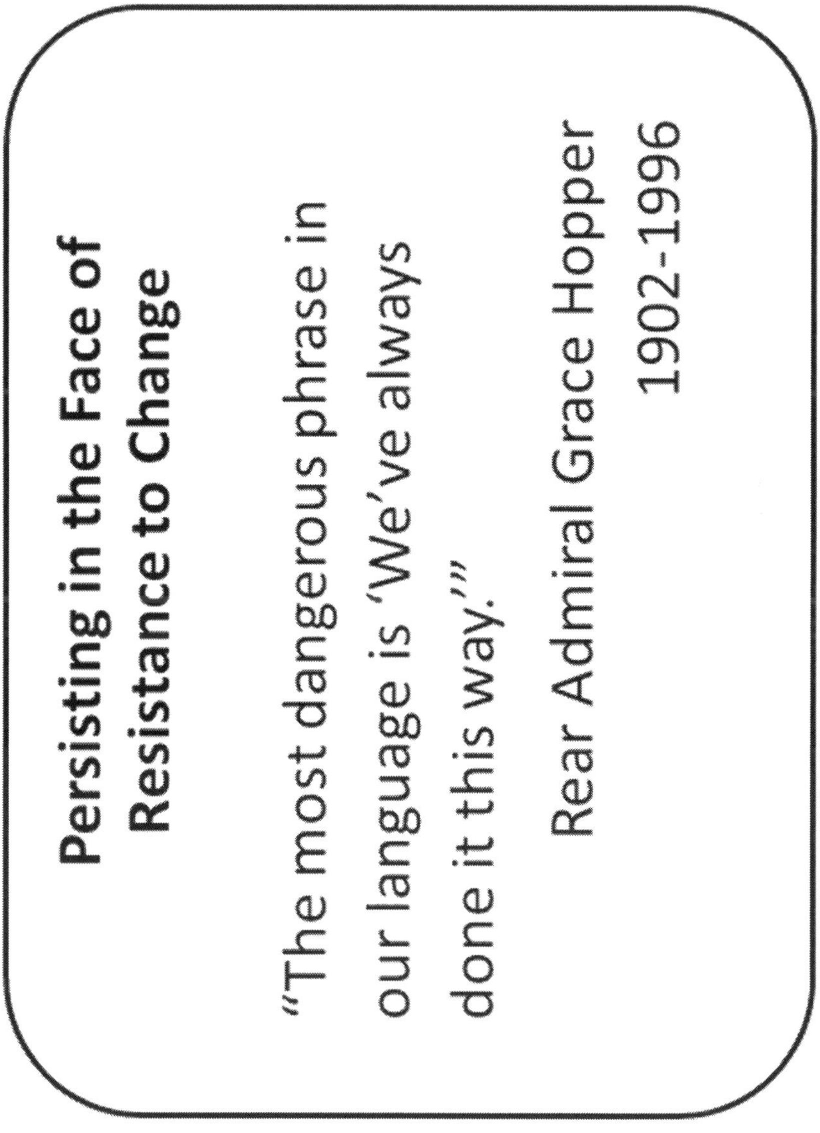

Persisting in the Face of Resistance to Change

"The most dangerous phrase in our language is 'We've always done it this way.'"

Rear Admiral Grace Hopper
1902-1996

Figure 5

Chapter 6
Where *DOES* All That Litter Come From?

We say that the litter we see in a ditch, caught by a fence, snagged in bushes or on a front lawn may have come from somewhere else. So where does all that litter come from?

Keep America Beautiful has long promoted a list of "7 major sources of litter" that has largely stood the test of time, proving useful and accurate since the mid-1970s. It has played a stalwart part in many successful local program designs.

Nonetheless, over three decades of field experience reveal that:

1. Almost 4 Americans in 10 now live in an apartment or townhouse community. So solid waste putout decisions made at multi-family communities need to be added.
2. Americans increasingly eat and recreate away from home. Decisions to litter at public places, special events, and entertainment venues, indoors and out, need to be addressed.
3. Finally, illegal littering in all of its often-remote locations was often discussed in early KAB System training but is not included on KAB's current major sources list. However, the scale and impact of illegal dumping on public health and water quality has significantly raised illegal dumping concerns...and potential educational program funding resources.
4. It is helpful to begin viewing the so-called "major sources of litter" not just as physical places where litter first happens, but as decision points where proper and improper solid waste management decisions are made. This lets us focus more on behaviors we can change rather than on physical situations, which can be harder to address.

5. Finally, it is also helpful to put the now ten (10) decision points into three categories that can help us in planning to attack the "low-hanging fruit" first.

These three categories are named Primary/Stationary, Secondary/Follow-On and Tertiary/Special.

While failure to retrieve loose debris and actual acts of littering certainly happen at the Primary Sources below, the core challenge tends to be that of promoting adequate containment that works for the property owner, resident, builder, etc. as well as sanitation workers, waste haulers and the community-at-large.

Primary Sources or Stationary Decision Points are the easiest to attack and often the largest generators of loose debris:

1. **Workplace Waste Putouts**
2. **Construction/Demolition Site Waste Handling**
3. **Loading/Receiving Docks Waste**
4. **Uncovered/Insecurely Loaded Vehicles**
5. **Single Family Residential Waste Putouts**
6. **Multifamily Community Putouts**

Taken together, these primary sources of litter are actually behavioral decision points where good and bad decisions about solid waste handling are made. They are stationary all or most all of the time. Being static, they are the easiest of all littering decision point locations to observe and to ticket or cite for code infractions.

Note: vehicles are best addressed when parked or stopped and they often have loads that add to litter because they are not covered or are poorly secured. This is not a passing concern as the AAA Foundation for Traffic Safety has found that hundreds of motorists and passengers are killed each year when their vehicles strike, or swerve to avoid, roadbed debris. Swerving matters as even doing so instinctively, to avoid a piece of blowing litter on a slick road, for example, can have lethal outcomes.

Secondary Decision Points are also labeled as "Follow-on Sources" because they describe highly mobile situations where the litterers are seeing the litter generated from the six primary sources and then deciding to add their litter to what is already there.

The four additional litter sources and decision points (Secondary and Special or Tertiary Sources) are discussed in Chapter 8.

NOTES:

Six Primary or Static Litter Decision Points

1. Workplace Waste Putout Points

2. Construction/Demolition Site Putout Points

3. Loading/Receiving Docks Putout Points

4. Uncovered Vehicles/Improperly Secured Loads

5. Single Family Residential Waste Putout Points

6. Multifamily Community Waste Putout Points

Figure 6

Chapter 7
Can't We Just Force Property Owners to Clean Up?

We can surely force an individual property owner to "clean up his or her own act" in response to a non-compliance situation. Many local ordinances require property owners to keep their properties clean and free of litter regardless of where that litter may have been generated. Code enforcement may in fact find that upwards of 80% or more of those they contact immediately correct problems that are brought to their attention.

Yet, persuading a property owner to clean up litter that started elsewhere, only to be thrown or blown onto their property, does not address the real litter generation problem. We may find that we are actually confronting, counseling and ticketing the victim!

An analysis of the litter at any particular property can help us determine which litter is being generated on-site and which may be coming from elsewhere. Understanding the forces that often move litter from one point to another, its dynamics, can help us pinpoint the place or places where inappropriate trash containment decisions are actually causing the litter we see.

The dynamics include:

- Wind
- Water
- Animals
- Vehicles

Using our knowledge of these dynamics when we perform assessments of the area surrounding our non-compliant neighbor can be very informative. Looking especially at the upwind and upstream areas, we can often identify the sources of litter that are victimizing our hapless citation target. This is important because educating him or her without also addressing the inadequate waste management practices of next door and across the street business and residential neighbors will not fully address the real problem. They too must be convinced to close their dumpsters, put trash out on the curb properly, keep their properties clean, etc.

NOTES:

Four Dynamics of Loose Litter That Move Trash from Place to Place

- Wind

- Water

- Animals

- Vehicles

Figure 7

Chapter 8
How About Those Other Four Litter Decision Points?

Secondary Sources of litter often get much of the blame for being "the cause of all that litter." In some cases as in retail parking lots, at many stop signs and public events, that blame may be appropriate. In many cases, however, these are "Me, too!" litterers. They are individuals who see litter generated by poor decision-making at one of the primary sources that has blown and gotten trapped nearby so they add their own litter to that which is already there. The unspoken assumptions are that "there is already litter there that someone else will be cleaning up sooner or later, so...." Consider that this is unlikely to be an isolated case because the litterer sees this sort of situation in many places.

Those two secondary/copycat decisions are those made by:

7. Motorists/Cyclists/Boaters/Ships and Their Passengers
8. Pedestrians/Walkers/Joggers/Bikers/Campers

An inordinate amount of time is often spent talking about and sometimes trying to do something about the littering decisions of motorists and pedestrians. Typically, this is done without first attacking Primary Decision Points and leads to little lasting success.

Motorists and Pedestrians are in some ways the most difficult of all targets to educate because they are on the move, they are very numerous, and addressing their containment needs is potentially very expensive.

The last kinds of littering are "Tertiary" or "Special" Litter Sources/Key Littering Decision Points. This category includes:

9. Sports, Entertainment and Recreational Sites (i.e. ball fields, movie theaters, beaches and riverfronts)
10. Illegal Dumping

Sports, Entertainment and Recreational Sites include venues such as sports arenas and movies seem to spawn a vicious interaction between hard-core "Me first is OK" litterers and "Me, too!" litterers. An exemplary site of this kind of littering is the former Texas Stadium, previously home to the Dallas Cowboys. There, littering was not spurred by construction trashing, business or home putout trashing, etc., yet it reportedly cost stadium management over $500,000 annually to clean up after events. In 2005, that was 25% more than TxDOT spent to clean the entire state highway right of way inside Irving's 69 square mile area.

Illegal Dumping is a grievous example of both Me First and Me Too littering, about which not enough is known. The working presumptions are that ignorance of laws and small business economics work to create and perpetuate illegal dumping. Little if any research exists on the actual values, triggers, and thinking of such litterers. No studies incorporating interviews, much less scientific focus interviews, with illegal dumpers could be found in the research done for this handbook. We suspect such interviews would confirm our belief that illegal dumper's actions reflect all the reasons that people would expect them to offer in justifying their behavior. However, having firsthand data would be helpful in preventing this practice and properly conducted focus groups can yield surprising results!

NOTES:

Four Secondary and Special Litter Decision Points

Secondary/Copycat Decision Points

7. Motorists, Cyclists, Boaters, Ships and Passengers

8. Pedestrians, Walkers, Joggers, Bikers, Campers

Tertiary/Special Decision Points

9. Public Event Venues and Sites
   (Ball fields, theaters, beaches, riverfronts, fairs, etc.)

10. Illegal Dumpsites/Dumpers

Figure 8

Organizational Questions

Chapter 9
What Are the Core Facts We Need to Know at the Local Level Before We Get Started?

There are two sources of facts about litter and littering that we do well to consider as we set out to win our local battles with litter, one community at a time. Those are external/global facts that we get from others and internal/local facts that we generate using tools and templates gained from our external fact-finding.

External/Global Facts

External/Global Facts encompass the research, facts and best practices we can glean from discoveries of what works and what does not, as proven by hundreds of other communities since the KAB System was first rolled out nationally in 1976.

1. These facts relate to fully understanding where litter starts, how to stop littering behavior, how such efforts are faring elsewhere, and how and when to best communicate information to our own community. These facts tells us WHAT works.

Internal/Local Facts

Other facts we need to determine are Internal/Local facts that we must gather in a systematic fashion and put to work locally. They will help us know HOW to put the KAB System to work in our community. This phase includes:

2. Listing our most influential associations and groups – and their leaders – in each sector of the community. This list should include every entity possible that is engaged in the process of solid waste containment and collection, recycling of consumer goods in particular, and public as well as private beautification activities. This enumeration should

include the local branch office of national KAB sponsors and branch offices of sponsors of our state office program.

3. Discovering the mission or purpose of each of these groups. (To bring about change through these groups, we must seek mission overlaps with our own mission.)

4. Researching written behavioral expectations that we have of one another, such as ordinances that specify rules about containing refuse properly, cleaning up loose refuse, not littering, recycling and beautifying.

5. Identifying and locating technology that is in use or available to help meet those expectations, including containment such as dumpsters and litter receptacles, clean up equipment and car litterbags. Expecting people to not litter from their cars without assuring that car litter bags are as available as any other disposable container such as leaf bags is probably not reasonable, for example.

6. Determining what educational materials are available that clarify the incentives for compliance with the written expectations and the disincentives for non-compliance.

7. Discovering how existing enforcement of litter laws, recycling regulations and beautification policies are being monitored and publicized. NOTE: A law that is perceived as poorly enforced can be even worse than no law at all.

8. Identifying what on-going education is happening in schools, workplaces, play places, and faith places in particular around litter, recycling, and beautification.

9. Recognizing both official and informal "subsets" of our community where people spend most of their non-work time is important. Communities of 50,000 and even smaller are not homogenous. People spend most of their lives in smaller circles of life that are largely described by the locations of their children's school, the personal services they repeatedly frequent, their church, etc. For example, if we ask a resident of Ourtown where they are from, they may well respond with a general reference to their present home state, "Ourstate," or their hometown, "Ourtown." But if you ask what part of Ourtown they live in, they are likely to start off by saying "north Ourtown," and, later, to share that their children attend school, they attend church and their parents live in "Las Vistas."

It is vital to understand these distinctions because, in the end, the KAB System works best where people feel a sense of community...and works less well where that sense of community is lacking. This person is telling you, regardless of the legend on some map or where they may office, that they actually live out their day-to-day life "in Las Vistas." We may need to begin thinking about a "Keep Las Vistas Beautiful" chapter program! A single program that seeks to serve all of Ourtown monolithically without reckoning with these "sense of community" realities is likely bound to enjoy more success in the press than on the streets.

Building upon this "community as a cluster of small villages" perspective, for communities of 50,000 or more (and even 25,000), we would be wise to conscientiously seek out community leaders in various areas of our affiliate to partner. Then we can train and support them as "micro affiliate coordinators" who can be of great help to us in reaching out to their areas of our town.

NOTES:

Core Facts We Need to Know Locally Before Getting Started

External/Global Facts

- Social aspects of values influencing littering
- Key attitudes surrounding littering/litter prevention
- Major litter control decision points
- Impacts of litter: physical, financial, etc.

Internal/Local Facts

- Baseline level of ambient/visual community litter
- Key leadership organizations and their leaders
- Litter related written expectations such as ordinances
- Availability of helping technology
- Existing economic rewards/penalties for compliance
- Presence of ongoing community education
- Public profile of existing enforcement efforts, if any

Figure 9

Chapter 10
Aren't My Friends and Acquaintances Who Believe in Our Mission Likely to Be the Best Board Members?

KAB affiliate boards are just like every other non-profit committee or board of directors. Ethnicity, gender, geography, skills, and networking balance all matter! However, their behavior change mission is unique. It is imperative that most affiliate board members be representatives from, not simply members of, their respective sectors, for it is through them that normative system change must be catalyzed.

They must...

Be Representative, meaning ideally that they have actually been sent to represent their community sector, not just members of those sectors. This is a subtle but highly important difference. Only the sent can truly represent!

There need to be representatives from the Business, Municipal Government, Neighborhoods, Multi-Family Community (Apartment), Schools, Youth Organization, and Communications/PR/Media Sectors. The primary roles of board members in a KAB affiliate program are a) assuring communications with sector leaders and b) promoting workshops in their sector that foster community-wide behavior change.

Be Capable, That is, able to recruit effectively for the local KABS organization the resources it needs along with the ability to manage those resources ethically and efficiently.

- **Be Truly Influential** within their respective community segments. The greatest KABS boards, in terms of their ability to foster lasting change, are NOT focused on overpowering or snookering others in order to persuade them or force them to take this or that course of short-term action. The greatest boards with the longest lasting legacies are those that discover the power of "working through existing organizations" and "working from the inside out."

For example, it is better over the long haul to have a board volunteer from the local Chamber of Commerce to help deal with the business community – one who speaks on behalf of and reports back to the Chamber-- rather than one who simply happens to be "a Chamber member." This goes in similar fashion for representatives from all the sectors named above here, and their sub-sectors. This aspect of board member service is only somewhat less true of the support committees such as special events, fund raising, etc.

There are exceptions to every rule, of course. But, usually, the best individuals are those who are influential within targeted, significant sub-sectors of the community.

So, are our friends and acquaintances necessarily our best board candidates? Maybe, maybe not. What do *you* think?

NOTES:

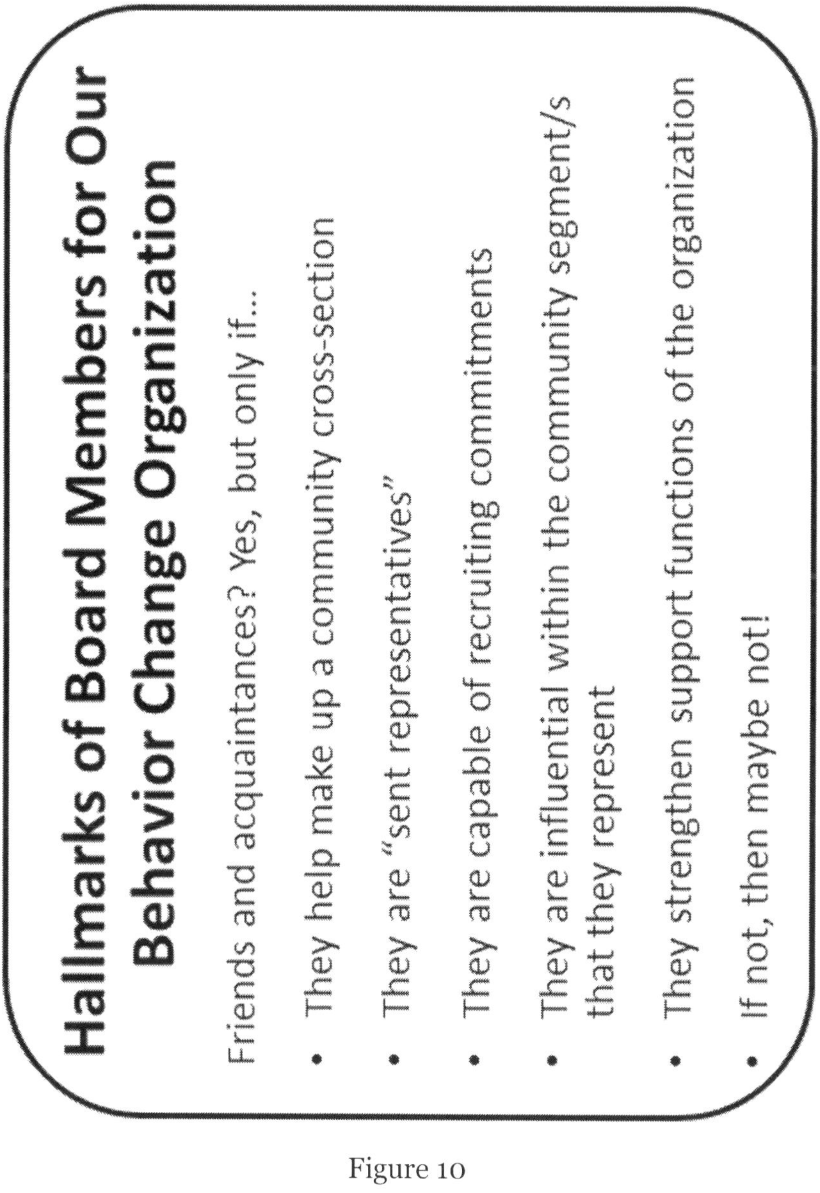

Hallmarks of Board Members for Our Behavior Change Organization

Friends and acquaintances? Yes, but only if...

- They help make up a community cross-section

- They are "sent representatives"

- They are capable of recruiting commitments

- They are influential within the community segment/s that they represent

- They strengthen support functions of the organization

- If not, then maybe not!

Figure 10

Chapter 11
OK, Who DOES Have to Be at The Table for Us to Be Effective?

Individuals who say that a local KABS program needs only a handful of committees (such as Cleanups, Fundraising, Awards, and Schools) MAY be correct for very small communities where everyone in town habitually and effectively wears many hats.

However, four out of five Americans live in metropolitan areas of 50,000 to 100,000 that, like KAB communities averaging 140,000, can benefit from having a more structured approach.

The most effective change strategies work from the inside out in each of six or seven major community sectors. Inside-out education is most effectively delivered in workshop settings where key participants learn to change the culture of their own "mini-communities." Committees are especially well suited to promoting such workshops across the community and the calendar each year.

Committees or clusters of functions keyed to those major sectors would likely include:

- Business/Industry/Labor
- Civic: Faith, Neighborhood, Service
- Media, Marketing/PR Firms
- Schools & Youth Groups: Public, Private, Local, National (Schools may meet separately from Youth Groups as the educational and youth service cultures can vary.)
- Government: Local, County, State, National
- Special Stakeholders: Waste Haulers, Recyclers, Nurseries, Tree and Plant Growers, etc.

The generic missions of these committees are fairly simple:

- Maintaining up-to-date lists of key groups and leaders in their respective area, including full contact information.
- Generating invitations for the local affiliate to make informational briefing presentations that can lead to longer, on-site workshops aimed at bring about lasting change for the better. A good house rule to adopt can be "Give NO Presentation Without Asking for a Commitment to Greater Engagement!"
- Following up presentations to schedule full Keep Ourtown Beautiful behavior change oriented workshops and better engage with Keep Ourtown Beautiful programming.
- Hosting scheduled workshops within their sectors.
- Nominating leading individuals and groups for community, state, and national recognition.
- Promoting sector-specific programs such as Green Builder, Green Campus, Green Apartments, Green Dumpster, Green Trucker, etc.

Note: "Greater Commitment" means asking, as appropriate, to present again in the future, to run added workshops, to volunteer on committees, to volunteer for special events and projects, to appoint liaisons to board or friends groups, and to provide generous funding.

NOTES:

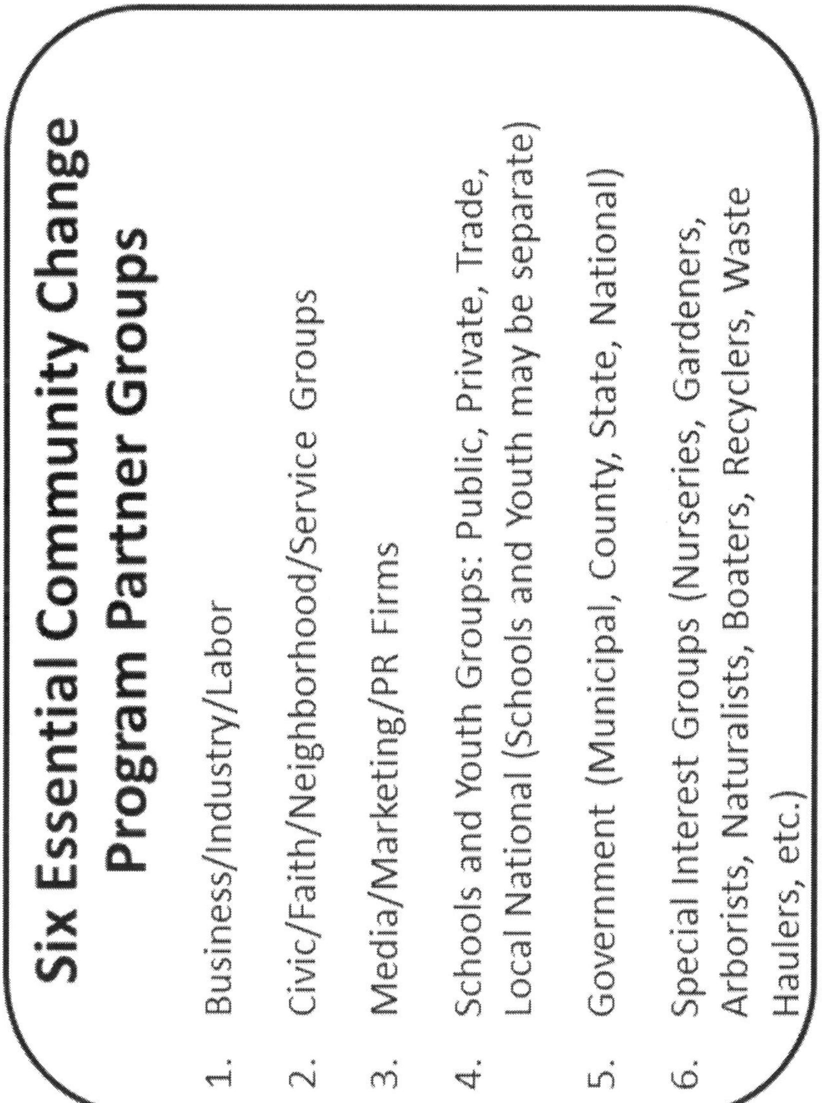

Six Essential Community Change Program Partner Groups

1. Business/Industry/Labor

2. Civic/Faith/Neighborhood/Service Groups

3. Media/Marketing/PR Firms

4. Schools and Youth Groups: Public, Private, Trade, Local National (Schools and Youth may be separate)

5. Government (Municipal, County, State, National)

6. Special Interest Groups (Nurseries, Gardeners, Arborists, Naturalists, Boaters, Recyclers, Waste Haulers, etc.)

Figure 11

Chapter 12
What Resources Will Our Organization Need to Be Effective Over Time?

As we saw in an earlier section covering the basic elements of managing complex change, local KABS programs -- regardless of whether they are public, private or not-for-profit – need core resources to be effective. These are sometimes called "capacity needs" or "capacity building needs." No less than any other economic development group, meeting these needs is a requirement if a KABS organization to perform at its highest and best level.

Academics, Research and Internships

Academics means keeping ourselves in front of the academic community and vice-versa. Our local KABS affiliate programs offer uniquely rich opportunities for students and professors to see how non-profits really work and how we foster and measure large-scale behavior change in the field.

Research simply means keeping in touch with academic and "trade" information articles, projects, data bases and findings that may help make ours a better organization and our organization better at managing and sustaining change.

Internships refers to our exchanging the service-learning experiences we can offer for the person power and brainpower that an intern can bring to us in ways that benefit them as students and us as program managers.

One caution: Our relationship with academia is NOT intended to "find a better way to fight litter, promote recycling, and support beautification." Rather, our academic relationships are intended to discover ways to strengthen our existing, long-proven KAB System behavior change program.

Culture change is a long-term process. Moreover, as is noted elsewhere in this manual, culture change programs often disappoint due to their failure to continually nourish leadership commitment, to consciously foster middle management buy-in, and to give "little people" the chances to be heard, be engaged in meaningful work, and be recognized. But, we know that the KAB System works when we work all of it!

Advocacy and Public Policy

All of us live in an ever-changing sea of local, state and national legislation that impacts the greater world of community service and our own world of solid waste education. Having at least one person monitoring legislative actions and nurturing relationships with elected and appointed policymakers is important and almost assuredly fruitful.

Development and Economic Analysis

Development means raising money and needed resources. This function helps the board meet its responsibility for acquiring the resources that the organization/group/program needs to pursue aggressively its missions of litter abatement, recycling enhancement, and beautification promotion. These resources may be "hard" such as cash or in-kind such as office space.

Economic Analysis means overseeing the annual cost-benefit analysis and "getting the word out" about the cost-effectiveness of our program. A new optional function for this group is that of conducting an annual "Litter Cost Impact Study." It is recommended that these studies be conducted on a rolling basis so that government statistics may be gathered the first year, schools sector statistics the second year, private sector statistics the third year and civic/neighborhood/non-profit statistics the fourth year (not necessarily in that order.) Such studies help local participants identify their cost of physically picking up litter and returning it to the proper waste handling process. These studies help us better estimate "the high cost of doing too little litter abatement." Along with the Cost-Benefit Analysis, they create an economic justification for continuing and expanding local KAB affiliate programs.

Continuous Quality Improvement (CQI)

The CQI function:

- Helps us generate reports to KAB, for our state office if any, for benefactors, and for others as needed.
- Produces the initial and follow-up Litter Index surveys.
- Conducts initial and follow-up Community Appearance Indexes/Focus Area Index reports.
- May produce the annual Community Attitude and Information Survey (recommended but not required).
- May help in conducting periodic Litter Cost Impact Studies.

Volunteer Management and Training

More even than money, volunteers are the engine that fuels community change programs. Even if a program's financial resources are considerable, it is people, individuals, who must work with other individuals to gain commitments to systematic change. The processes of identifying, recruiting, orienting and training, placing, supervising, motivating, recognizing, and retaining volunteers add up to a BIG job! This function should not be left up solely to paid or senior staff. The board president or other designated board member needs to be involved in carrying out all of these volunteer management functions!

COMMENT: Even larger communities may not have an individual or committee for every function noted above. *HOWEVER*, the functions and needs noted in Figure 12.2 must be clearly addressed to support the strongest possible behavior change program

NOTES:

Five Essential Community Change Program Support Functions

1. Academics, Research and Service-Learning Internships

2. Advocacy and Public Policy

3. Development and Economic Analysis

4. Continuous Quality Improvement
   - Reports for KAB, KOurStateBeautiful, Benefactors
   - Annual Litter Index
   - Community Appearance Index (Very Helpfull!)
   - Litter Cost Analysis (Optional but Crucial)

5. Volunteer Management and Training

Figure 12.1

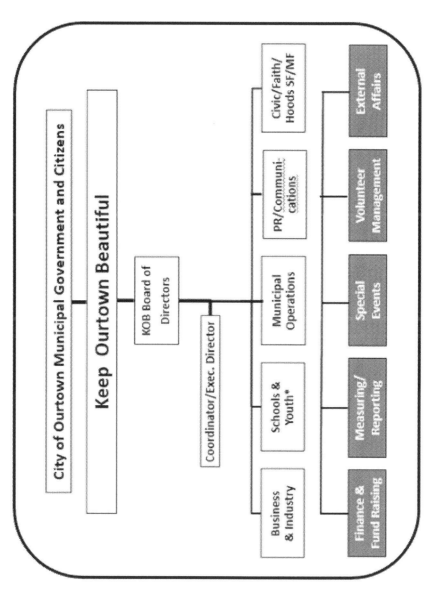

Figure 12.2

Chapter 13
Can You Tell Me a Little More About Acquiring the Money and Person power That We Will Need?

Of course, money first. Like it or not, raising the money required to pursue an organization's mission is the core duty of every board, whether for-profit or not-for-profit. Period. Virtually every board and every board member is responsible for meeting this obligation one way or another. Period. Yet, a large percent of the board members on a large percent of all boards, perhaps including our own, avoid fund raising as if it was the Ebola virus.

So, what are some steps we can take?

First, we can do some re-wording of our Bylaws and/or operating procedures as well as our board member job descriptions. We can assure that they include a phrase such as "I commit to personally aid in reaching out to existing and potential funders, as well as in-kind support providers, to offer them the opportunity to help assure the financial soundness of our organization." We can use our Board and our lawyers if we have them to individualize this language as needed.

Second, we can stop talking about "the ask." Our relations with potential funders are truly ones where we are not asking but offering. We are helping philanthropists reach their typical goals of supporting healthy, financially secure, high quality communities.

Remember: We are Offering an Opportunity, Not Begging for a Handout!

Our particular kinds of programs offer:

- A unique opportunity to increase the leverage of donors' investments with our 1:3 to 1:16 average cost-benefit experience.
- A unique opportunity to help the community prevent the blight of litter while promoting recycling and beautification pro-actively instead of reactively.
- A unique opportunity to bring the entire community together in a way than teaches us all better ways to manage other community behavioral challenges.

Third, we should have our Development and Economic Analysis function in place to handle our fund raising guidance tasks. This group should be organizing to compete for KAB's many grant opportunities as well as for local grants and corporate gifts.

Fourth, before we present opportunities, we can make sure we are prepared by having the following in hand:

NOTE: The list below is Non-Profit oriented but applies in principal to governmental agencies as well. Semper Paratus!

1. State tax-exempt status: current state certification.
2. EIN#, DUNS#, approved sales tax exemption form.
3. IRS tax-exempt status: federal 501(c)(3) letter...both printed and electronic. A fully completed application to the IRS is okay if that is all you have but some funders cannot give you support until you have your letter of approval from IRS. Having filed as a state level non-profit corporation is likely not enough...but asks as you go along, one prospect at a time!
4. Form 990: previous year's tax form from accountant or bookkeeper, if available.
5. Articles of Incorporation.
6. Vision statement: agency's board approved statement of purpose and goals.
7. Mission statement: agency's board approved statement of purposed activities (in general) to pursue that vision.
8. Goals: What we hope to achieve over the next 2 to 5 years.
9. Bylaws: current and up-to-date.
10. Current board members list: names, contact information, professions, affiliations, and current terms
11. Most recent audited financial statement: previous year's report from accountant or bookkeeper, if available.

12. Program budget: report from accountant or bookkeeper, if available.
13. Project budget: specific to present proposal.
14. Qualifications of paid or pro bono executive director: curriculum vitae, background, accomplishments, degrees.
15. Qualifications of pertinent staff: cv for personnel who will oversee or participate significantly in the specific project.
16. Letters of support: community leaders, funders, etc.
17. Program evaluation statistics on persons served: who, what, when, where, how and so what?
18. Agency background information: brochures, accomplishments, projects, newspaper articles, etc. if appropriate.
19. Guide Star listing and Volunteer Match listing
20. Trade association memberships: KAB, state KAB office, state recycling program, EPA, state environmental agency, volunteer management association, etc.
21. Registration with area volunteer center, center for non-profit management, Chamber, council of governments, etc.
22. Statement of Commitment of Board, i.e., "100% of our board members, without exception, have made appropriate financial contributions to support our mission within the past year."

Fifth, as collection of the documents above and completion of action items is progressing, another important four tasks can be taken up that focus on establishing or upgrading our reputation.

Reputation development begins with reputation determination. We need to know what others with the power to help fund our program think of us! These are hard and perhaps intimidating tasks but they can also prove to be of great benefit to us!

1. We Should Meet With Three *Existing Funders*, Ask Them How They *Really* Think We Are Doing...Remember (REM): Be Still, Listen, Write it Down.
2. We Should Meet With Three Potential *Corporate Funders*, Ask Them How Fundable They Think We Are/Could Become...REM: Be Still, Listen, Write It Down.
3. Meet With Three Potential **Charitable Funders**, Ask Them How Fundable They Think We Are/Could Become...REM: Be Still, Listen, Write It Down.

4. Meet With Three Potential **_Public Funders_**, Ask Them How Fundable They Think We Are/Could Become...REM: Be Still, Listen, Write It Down.

About Active Listening: There is no rule during the above interviews that is more important or potentially vital than "Be Still, Listen, Write It Down. Silence really can be golden and it's crucial that we ask our question, stop, and be still until they finish sharing. No defensiveness, no explaining, no clarifying unless asked for and then in 20 seconds or less. None! Just ask for permission to take notes then do so...only. You can ask for clarification for yourself but carefully: Could you tell us a little more about _____? Do you have a time frame in mind for _____? Is there someone you might suggest we talk to about _____? Where do you suggest that we might find _____? NEVER ask for a justification of any kind regarding the opinions, insights or judgments you have been offered! Clarification, yes; justification, no. If you do, you may never get the chance again.

Sixth, finally and completely separate from the fact-finding exercise above, we simply must focus on "Just Offer!" The single greatest reason that organizations, including affiliates like ours, do not get more support is the failure to offer...to present opportunities to invest to others...and offer, and offer, and offer!

As for volunteers, we also have a Volunteer Management and Training committee or function noted in Chapter 12.

This group should be working to fill the volunteer needs of the office staff, of other committees, of special events and perhaps to support the boards Nominating Committee.

They do not need all the documents assembled by the Development group, but they should have access to those documents. Asking the chair of the volunteer committee to come along on visits with potential donors and on annual donor calls is a smart move. Donors l-o-v-e to hear from volunteers, if their sharing is as brief and informative as it is enthusiastic!

The first duties of the Volunteer group are to assess the volunteer needs of the program from top to bottom. We need them to create thumbnail, at least, job descriptions of key volunteer positions, both long-term and part-time or temporary. Clue: Googling "How to write a volunteer job description" or "How to write a service-learning proposal" can be very helpful and save time.

Sources of volunteers include:

- Friends, family, and workmates of existing volunteers.
- The employees and volunteers of cooperating organizations.
- Volunteers solicited through our own organization's social media network.
- Volunteer job postings with area high schools. elementary school PTA's, and colleges.
- Youth and sports associations.
- Job postings with our local volunteer center.
- Our municipal court system (community service in lieu of fine payments).
- Student service organizations such as Phi Theta Kappa, the international service society of the two-year college (potentially super help and long lasting).
- Service-learning coordinators at high schools, community colleges and universities can be extremely helpful (We need to LISTEN to their goals and agendas then suggest ways that working together can help meet their need.)
- Listings on Volunteer Match (www.volunteermatch.org) and perhaps other online listing services.

Volunteer management wisdom informs us that a large percentage of all volunteers do so, initially at least, simply because they have been asked. So...offer!!

Thus, the funds we do not have and the volunteer person power we do not have may often be lacking for one common reason...a simple failure on our part to offer opportunities and even just asking plainly for help.

This simple rubric can help in recruiting resources of all kinds: Research, Prepare, Show Value, Offer, and Thank Warmly and Often.

NOTES:

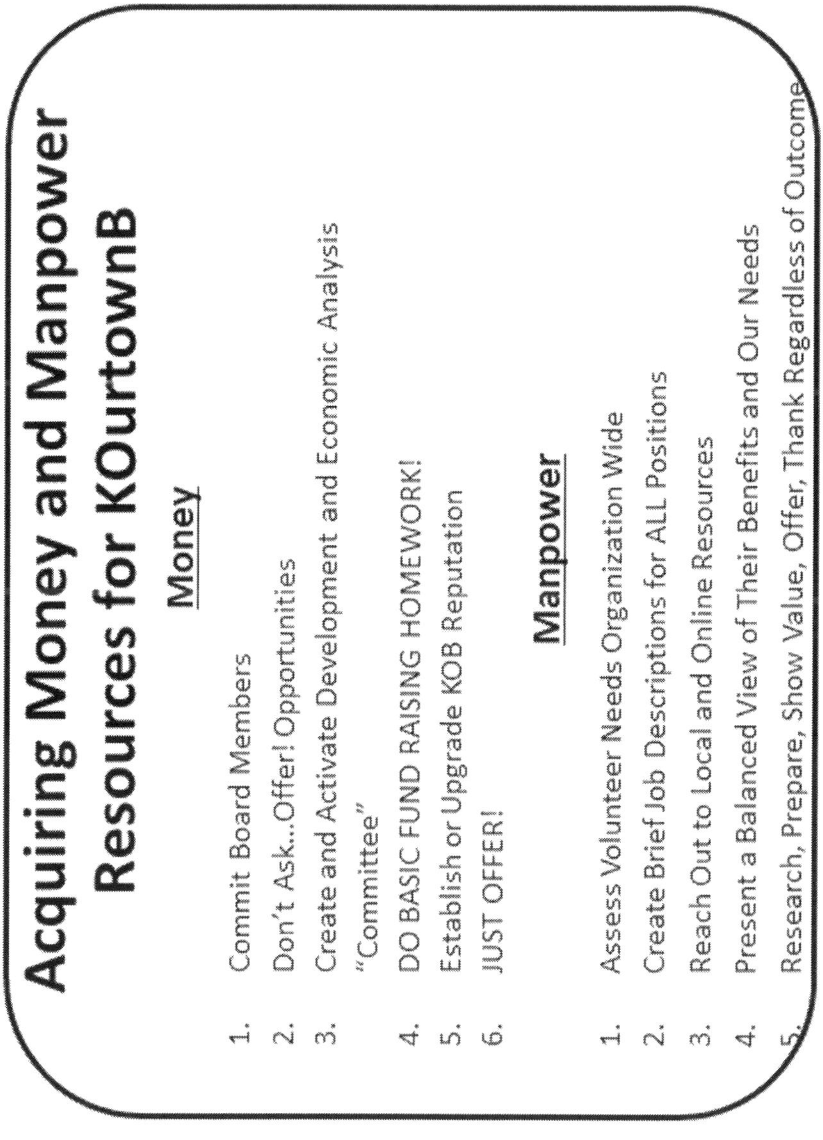

Acquiring Money and Manpower Resources for KOurtownB

Money

1. Commit Board Members
2. Don't Ask...Offer! Opportunities
3. Create and Activate Development and Economic Analysis "Committee"
4. DO BASIC FUND RAISING HOMEWORK!
5. Establish or Upgrade KOB Reputation
6. JUST OFFER!

Manpower

1. Assess Volunteer Needs Organization Wide
2. Create Brief Job Descriptions for ALL Positions
3. Reach Out to Local and Online Resources
4. Present a Balanced View of Their Benefits and Our Needs
5. Research, Prepare, Show Value, Offer, Thank Regardless of Outcome

Figure 13

Chapter 14
What Are Key Elements of a Good, Simple Project Plan?

While the specifics of a project action plan may gradually change over time and from project to project, the basic elements can be outlined in the simple terms below. Organizing resource acquisition and project planning along timelines for these factors makes success much more likely. A successful project likely starts early to line up and write out the following:

- (A Clear) Mission and Goals.
- Responsibility.
- Money.
- Person power.
- Materials, Tools, Equipment, Facilities
- Information.
- Authority.
- Time/Timeline, (Draft early, update often!)

(A Clear) Mission and Goals: As we have seen elsewhere here, clarity of mission is critical. Everyone involved in the activities of an affiliate need to be clear on the common and agreed upon mission, goals, and methods of the organization. REM: *Some ONE person* needs to have primary **responsibility** for carrying out a program or project.

Money: Sufficient funds are an obvious requirement. Projects often go forward without waiting to gather sufficient funds. When we do, we risk burning out and losing valuable staff as well as key volunteers.

Person power: Of all the resources listed here, the need for sufficient person power for each task and project cannot be over emphasized. Asking staff and key volunteers to repeatedly carry a workload more appropriately handled by far more people is a key factor in the burnout and loss of those the affiliate can least afford to go forward without.

Materials, Tools, Equipment, Facilities to get the job done as right as possible are needed. It is a fact of legendary proportions that "non-profits throw people at problems where corporations and governments tend to throw money at them." A result of this practice is that volunteers and staff spend truly inappropriate amounts of person power to get "free" donated materials, tools, etc. However, spending 2 hours to drive across town and back plus gas to get 25 pounds of "free" hamburger that must be kept frozen until just before an event when it can be bought nearby for $31.25 ready to cook is rarely a good deal!

Information: Lack of information, or more often access to information, is a major hampering factor for many non-profits. Our board members should be making every effort to get needed mailing lists, contact information, and other community data. This avoids asking staff and key volunteers to a) spend untoward amounts of time trying to get needed information or b) do a first class job with third class information. Additionally, letting information sources off the sharing hook denies them beneficial "buy in" opportunities.

Authority: A lack of authority, whether the product of ordinance language or the lack of a memo from a City Manager, can greatly handicap our affiliate's capacity to battle litter and promote recycling. It is up to our affiliate Board President or committee chair to assure that authority shortfalls are prevented or cured. If a president or chair is encountering stiff resistance, it is likely time for a full executive committee or even the entire board to show up in the City Manager's office...or the Mayor's office...in addition to the offices of each board member's individual council representative. The power of motivated, organized voters can rarely be matched by staff, especially if the senior affiliate paid staff person (coordinator) is a City employee.

Time/Timeline. This resource merely urges that a written timeline for projects be created and that committing to unreasonable or Herculean deadlines be avoid. Such deadlines increase stress and greatly increase the chance that a lot of hard work will earn disappointments and resentments.

Note: See also the "Mission Keeper Form" that is described in Chapter 21.

Proper Prior Participative Planning Predictably Promotes Prideful, Provable Performance

NOTES:

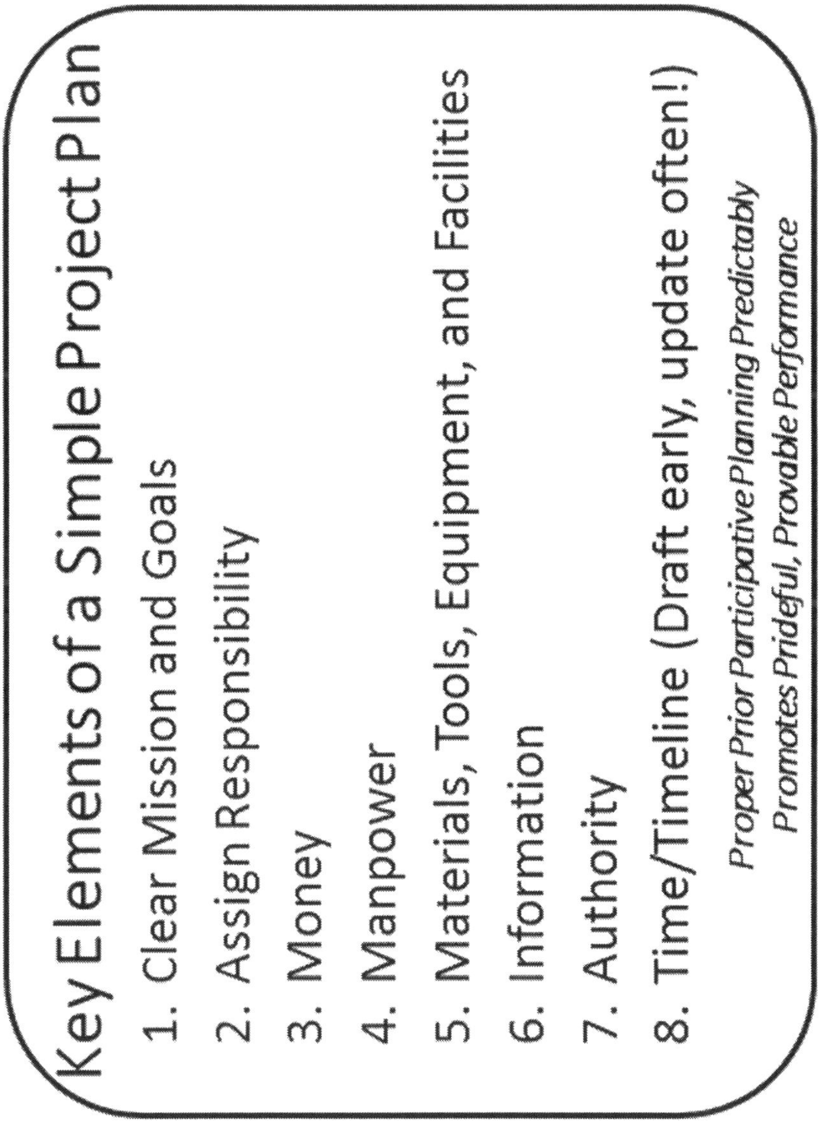

Key Elements of a Simple Project Plan

1. Clear Mission and Goals
2. Assign Responsibility
3. Money
4. Manpower
5. Materials, Tools, Equipment, and Facilities
6. Information
7. Authority
8. Time/Timeline (Draft early, update often!)

Proper Prior Participative Planning Predictably
Promotes Prideful, Provable Performance

Figure 14

Chapter 15
What Organizing Steps Should We Take to Be Effective?

The KABS has an extraordinary record of accomplishment in large part because its simple, 5-step strategic change scheme is quite similar to the basic elements of many well-known, time-tested management change strategies. Labels change, but the underlying functions they describe vary far less.

Some confusion has occurred since the initial rollout of the KAB System in the mid-1970s. The passage of time and the practice of sound bite messaging have brought many to refer repeatedly to "the five step KAB behavior change process." This is a bit of a misnomer for these five steps describe simple, classic management steps. The management of almost any activity or group can be initiated using these steps:

- **Get the Facts.**
- **Engage ALL the Stakeholders** and especially their leaders.
- **Plan Systematically**.
- **Focus on Results.**
- **Provide Positive Reinforcement**.

While these steps alone are not intended to form a behavioral change program, they become extremely powerful when integrated with KAB's behavioral management steps which are discussed in the next chapter.

This KAB variant of Dr. Robert Allen's Normative System Culture Change Process is has been widely deployed and proven in the field. Its documented success earns numerous accolades.

It is:

- Locally-owned and -operated.
- Consistently systematic across hundreds of communities.
- Highly cost-benefit focused.
- Sustainable.
- Sustained for almost 40 years.
- Cross transferable to other human behavior challenges.

The KAB System story, beginning in 1974, is one of vastly under-appreciated and under-recognized social change achievement.

The tale of its growth as an applied behavior change experiment, really, that began in three southeastern United States communities is remarkable. The KABS is now practiced in over 600 local communities in 41 states, and 24 of those states have official state offices. It is a saga that has much to teach us about dealing with all manner of community behavior challenges. For more on the cross-applicability power of the KAB System, see Chapter 29.

NOTES:

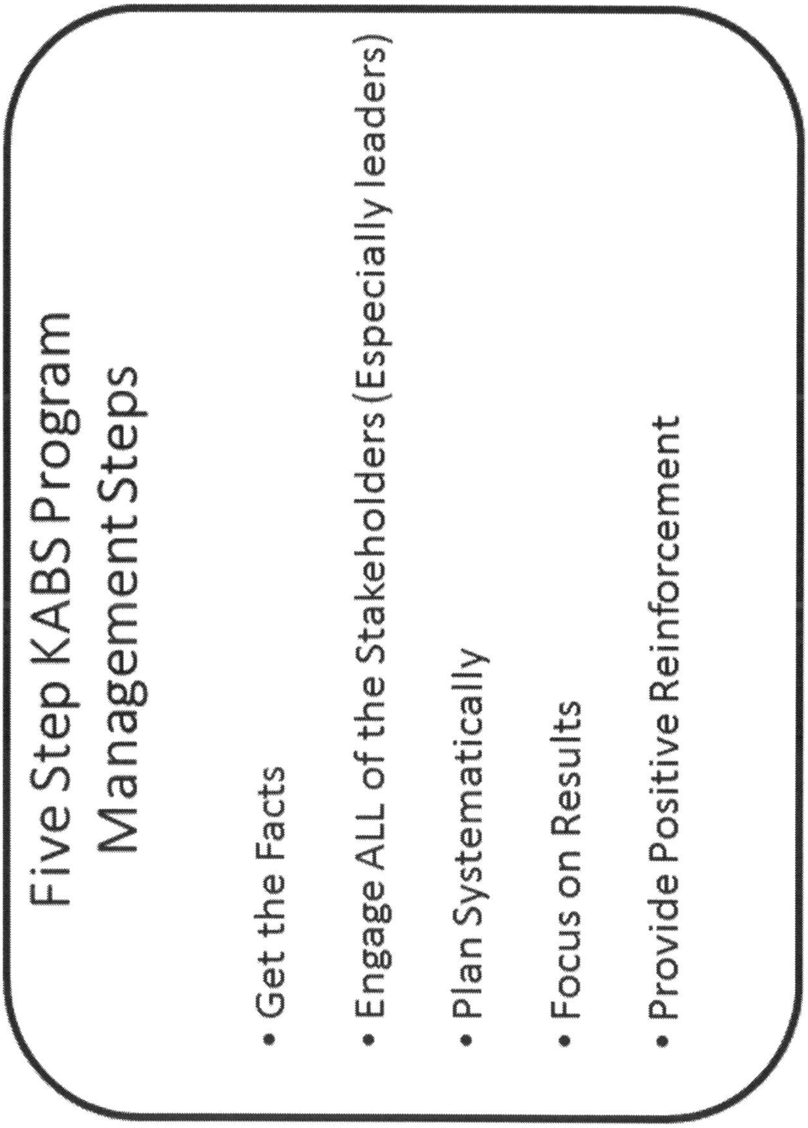

Five Step KABS Program Management Steps

- Get the Facts
- Engage ALL of the Stakeholders (Especially leaders)
- Plan Systematically
- Focus on Results
- Provide Positive Reinforcement

Figure 15

Program Design and Execution Questions

Chapter 16
How DO We Change People's Attitudes (and Behaviors)?

"Get the Facts" gets most of the glory when the KAB System is mentioned. However, it is its five behavior management strategies (formerly known as "pressure points" that actually work together to coach a community's pro-litter normative social system into becoming a litter abating normative culture instead.

The five behavior management strategies are addressed below. Caution is offered that, taken together, these strategies constitute a complete system, a recipe for lasting success. Taken 1, 2 or even 3 at a time without relevance to one another, they become just a list of exercises, akin to a partial list of recipe contents. The phrase, "Clarified Positive and Negative Consequences" may seem new to some, but its significance has always been a part of on-going conversations about practicing the KAB System.

Upgraded Written Expectations: Upgraded written expectations, whether in the form of ordinances or other formal rules, document our written expectations of one another. They lay out consequences for non-compliance and describe how those expectations may be reinforced. The process of building consensus around their wording may challenge us but also rewards us with understanding and bonding not otherwise readily available. Gaining final adoption of upgraded written expectations also allows us to renew the commitments of elected and appointed officials, management and our leaders. Their approval of changes in expectations such as those embedded in ordinance updates is usually required and always a key to our success.

Improved Technology: Increased helping technology makes written expectations more reasonable. Better dumpsters, more litter and trash receptacles, readily available car litterbags, etc. all help us obey reasonable laws and other written expectations.

Clarified Positive and Negative Consequences: Most human behavior is "conditioned." We choose behavior that rewards us and avoid behavior that penalizes us. When consequences are clear, they help us choose productive behavior and prevent our becoming clients of the local enforcement process.

On-going Education: The simple yet challenging job of education, especially of the adult population, is to let us know about ordinances, about helping technology, about economic consequences, and about enforcement we may encounter.

Effective Enforcement: Enforcement should only be required in the 5%-10% of cases where the other four strategies fail to get desired behavior changes. The high public profile of regular, even-handed enforcement activity is an essential ingredient in the "power mix" of all the other strategies. Experience suggests that laws that are not known to be enforced may as well not exist at all, in the minds of some.

Kurt Lewin, the father of modern social psychology, might have graphed our change strategies as driving and resisting forces with the centerline representing the "new normal."

Driving Forces	→	←	Resisting Forces
Drive for Improved Ordinances	→	←	Legal Department Understaffed
Drive for Improved Helping Technology	→	←	Streets Resisting Servicing More Containers
Drive for Clarifying Consequences	→	←	Court Fines Consistently Low
Drive to Provide More Public Education	→	←	Storm Water/KOB Competition
Drive to Show Higher Enforcement Profile	→	←	Police and Code Enforcement Disinterest

NOTES:

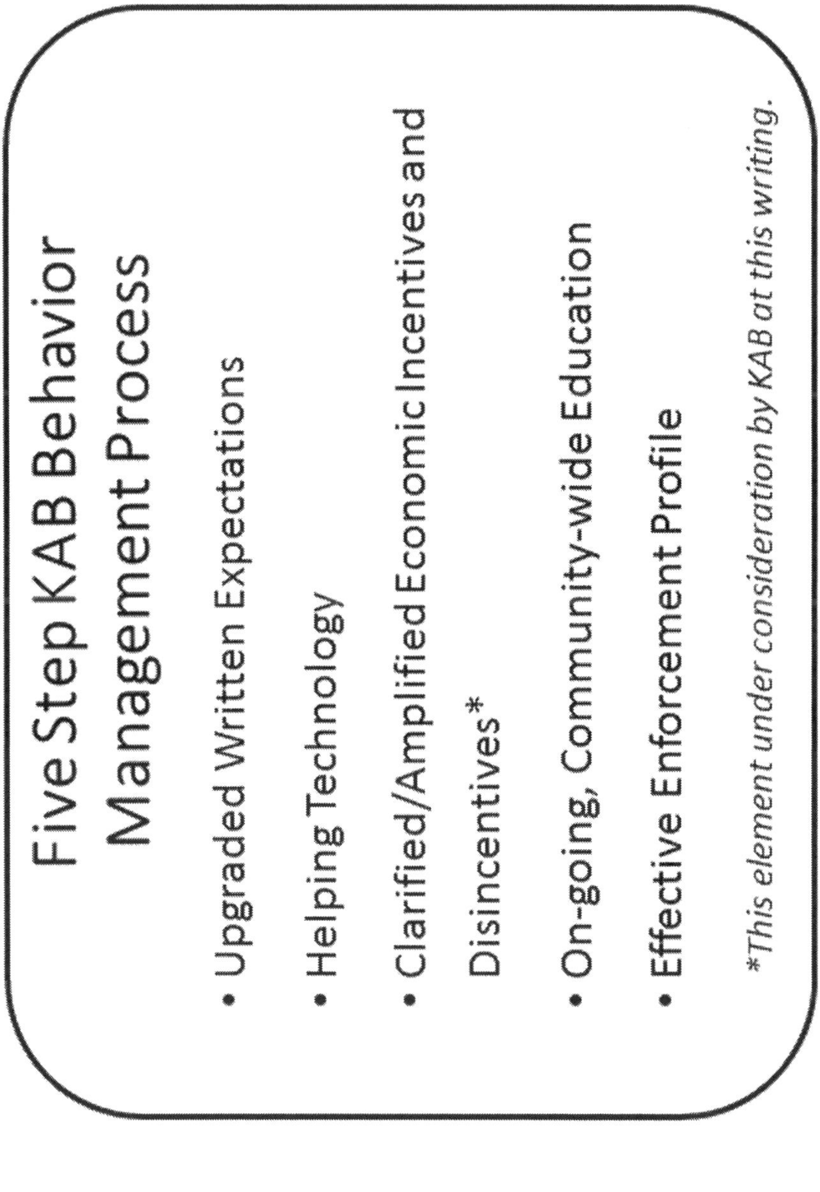

Five Step KAB Behavior Management Process

- Upgraded Written Expectations

- Helping Technology

- Clarified/Amplified Economic Incentives and Disincentives*

- On-going, Community-wide Education

- Effective Enforcement Profile

*This element under consideration by KAB at this writing.

Figure 16

Chapter 17
Isn't More Public Education the Key to Our Long-term Success?

Absolutely! Public education is likely our most powerful culture change tool...*provided* that is working hand-in-hand with the other elements of the KAB System. The capacity of education that is working independently to bring about lasting change for the better? Probably not so much. "Just Say No!" has had little impact. "Tobacco Kills" has left us with 1 in 5 adult Americans still smoking. The much-beloved "Don't Be a Litterbug" campaign that began in 1953 has not left us with a clean America.

To maximize its effectiveness, education must echo and reinforce basic KAB System precepts.

- Education should inform recipients what laws (written expectations) exist that set out our responsibilities for proper solid waste disposal.
- Education should inform participants about helping technology that can make compliance with those written expectations reasonable and as easy as possible.
- Education should clarify the rewards of compliance with written expectations as well as the potential penalties of non-compliance.
- Education should point out the breadth and scale of educational efforts community-wide so that those being informed are aware that they are not the only ones being asked to change their behavior.
- Finally, Education should inform those being educated of any and all enforcement being done in **both** the public and private sectors, as much as possible.

If community education does not make clear and sequential reference to the other community KAB System program efforts, it may, in fact, conflict with and lessen the impact of those efforts.

In short, the power of environmental education is largely defined by the strength of the educational environment in which it is presented. As Judith Landau-Stanton and her colleague, Collen D. Clement, put it in their book, AIDS, Health and Mental Health, in 1990, "Sociological studies confirm that an individual's behavior can be altered only if the systems in which that individual works and lives support the change. If those systems are not supportive, and are not altered, the individual will, at best, experience frustration in his or her attempts to exhibit the new behavior and, at worst, not attempt to change at all."

In the following diagram, we see that the outer ring of building a supportive green education environment is labeled Written Expectations. These can be ordinances, operating guides, standard operating procedures, company rules, etc. The KAB System recommends that all written expectations **include** stakeholder input and have management's approval and backing. Written expectations specify what is accepted and expected behavior. They often make reference to helping technology and may describe penalties for non-compliance

Second is "Helping Technology." This refers not just to newer, fancier technology in general, but specifically to technology (or information) that facilitates or makes it easier to comply with ordinances. For example, the expectation that everyone is to put their properly contained and secured trash out at curbside on a particular morning of the week is facilitated by the city's sending out emailed or text reminders the day before pickups are scheduled and providing sturdy, wheeled trash bins to all residents. Similarly, compliance with a ban on littering from autos is made easier if car litter bags are available at local stores or fire stations.

The third element in our educational environment is that of providing economic incentives and disincentives. This means, for example, explaining the benefits of minimizing neighborhood and business litter. It also means emphasizing potential fines resulting from non-compliance and taking care of waste containers to prevent being fined for their damage or loss.

Our fourth element in this example is Enforcement Presence. Enforcement staffers are very familiar with the fact that their uniforms, behavior, and even physical stance project an expectation of compliance with laws and of penalties for infractions. Their very presence communicates that a) laws exist and b) they are being enforced. Without this presence in the community, it is as if formal laws and law enforcement around a particular community issue do not exist in any meaningful way.

Tight budgets and local issues often leave litter law enforcement well down on the list of enforcement activity. Therefore, every possible step should be taken to maximize the public profile, the tangible presence, of enforcement. Awards to and recognition of enforcement staff, publicizing the number of citations written, citations arbitrated, and fines levied all promote the all-important "presence factor."

Our fifth and final element is on-going, community-wide education. This diagram represents the hard-earned philosophy that, to be most effective, education must:

- Reflect and reinforce written expectations.
- Reflect and reinforce the existence of helping technology.
- Reflect and reinforce economic incentives for compliance and disincentives for non-compliance.
- Reflect and reinforce the presence of enforcement.
- Be on-going year-round since litter generation is happening daily, weekly, monthly...year-round.
- Be community-wide as litter generation is happening in every sector – public, private and civic – community wide.

NOTES:

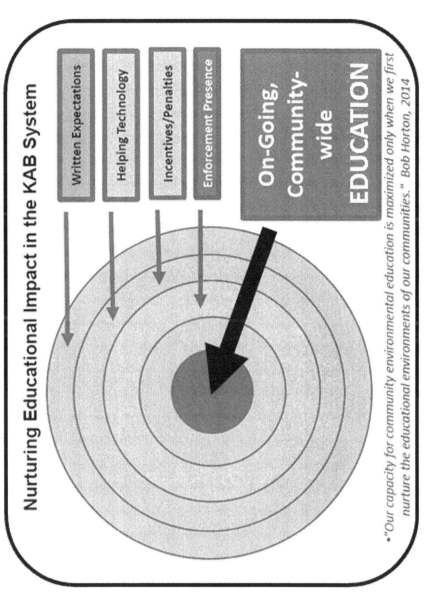

Figure 17

Chapter 18

We Are Easily the Most Active Program We Know of In Our Area; Shouldn't That Get Us the Results We Want and Need?

Your activism is no doubt generating results. But, consider this scenario...

The Our Keep Ourtown Beautiful program year has come to an end. We have again entered all our final operating statistics. As we press the print key, our Board President drops by the office. We go together to the printer to get a quick look at our results.

As the report prints out, our Board President blanches. Her face white, she turns to us and asks, "How can our litter be going up?"

We sit down together and go over the report. One by one we look at the volunteer recruiting, volunteer service hours, number of events, trash collected, and recyclables collected. All are up and even donations and press coverage improved in a tough year. We can be proud of that we tell her. Unfortunately, our Board's attention to the five primary behavior change strategies specified by our KAB System has tapered off steadily. Focus has been, instead, on activity-related activities that have been fun and gotten good press coverage while generating the statistics in our annual report. In addition, we have won awards and recognition for our efforts, too!

Our board chair, a solid, goal-oriented leader, takes a seat. "I see," she says, "that we need to pay a lot more attention to the input you as our professional staff have been offering about working the KAB System behavior change strategies. We need to get back to those if we are going to reach our litter reduction goals. Let's start by looking again at our Focus Area Survey and Litter Index. I will NOT have litter growing on my watch!"

We breathe a sigh of relief that all along the way we have been documenting both our efforts and our results. We agree when she suggests that we draft an updated action plan, run it by our state office and KAB then take it to the board, our City Manager and the mayor, right after the holidays.

So, our regular and objective reporting on program activity and measured impact serves us well. For more on the subject, we can also review our KAB manuals and review "Measuring Outcomes of United Way–Funded Programs: Expectations and Reality," studies conducted by United Way.

http://web.pdx.edu/~stipakb/download/PA555/OutcomeMeasur ementAtUnitedWay.pdf

NOTES:

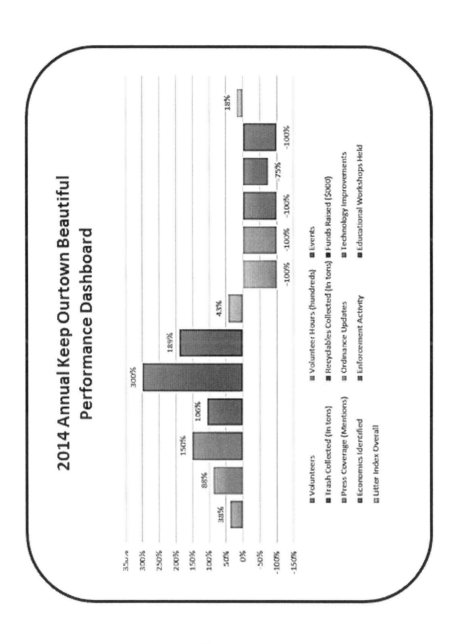

Figure 18

Chapter 19
What Are the Basic Elements of an Effective Litter Law Digest?

It is felt by some that "Everyone knows that there are laws against littering. People should just obey them." This is incorrect as many and perhaps most people do *not* know what litter is or what the law is and such statements fail to address the many challenges of enforcing litter laws. Plus, the motorists and pedestrians who are most often the targets of these statements are quite often not the major contributors to litter in many specific situations. Secondly, actually observing litterers in the act can be time-consuming and frustrating as even the most active of litterers does not litter every time, all the time. Finally, even if I see *you* litter and report it, we could easily find ourselves in front of a frustrated judge who hears me say you did litter and hears you protest that you did not. If I cannot prove convincingly that you littered, then you remain innocent until proven guilty. Proven!

Does this mean we should just give in to littering? No, of course not. But to improve our chances of becoming more effective believers that a cleaner city is a better city, we'll need to step up our game. A key part of that stepping up is to create a "Litter Laws Digest."

Such a digest is made up of five inter-related elements that must all be in place for a digest to be really useful:

1. The inclusion of all ten primary, secondary and tertiary decision points where littering happens.
2. Language addressing all three potential modes of litter generation and persistence (improper containment, failure to retrieve/clean up, and the act of littering).

3. Clear and specific penalties for littering, for allowing litter to remain uncontained, i.e., on the ground, and failure to properly contain solid waste to prevent it becoming litter.
4. Enforcing agency name(s) and contact information.
5. Specific requirements for a complaint to be as easy to address as is possible such as day, date, time, location, etc.

Whatever format such a pamphlet or poster might take, it will be important to distribute it widely to all of the decision points where proper solid waste containment can be achieved and loose litter be retrieved. "All" in this case means every workplace, learning place, faith place, living place whether single family home or multi-family community, church, etc. Secondly, it must be kept current with, perhaps, updates being emailed periodically and the most up-to-date version being on a municipal web page. Fresh looking, informational materials teach best and reflect well on sponsors and our program.

NOTES:

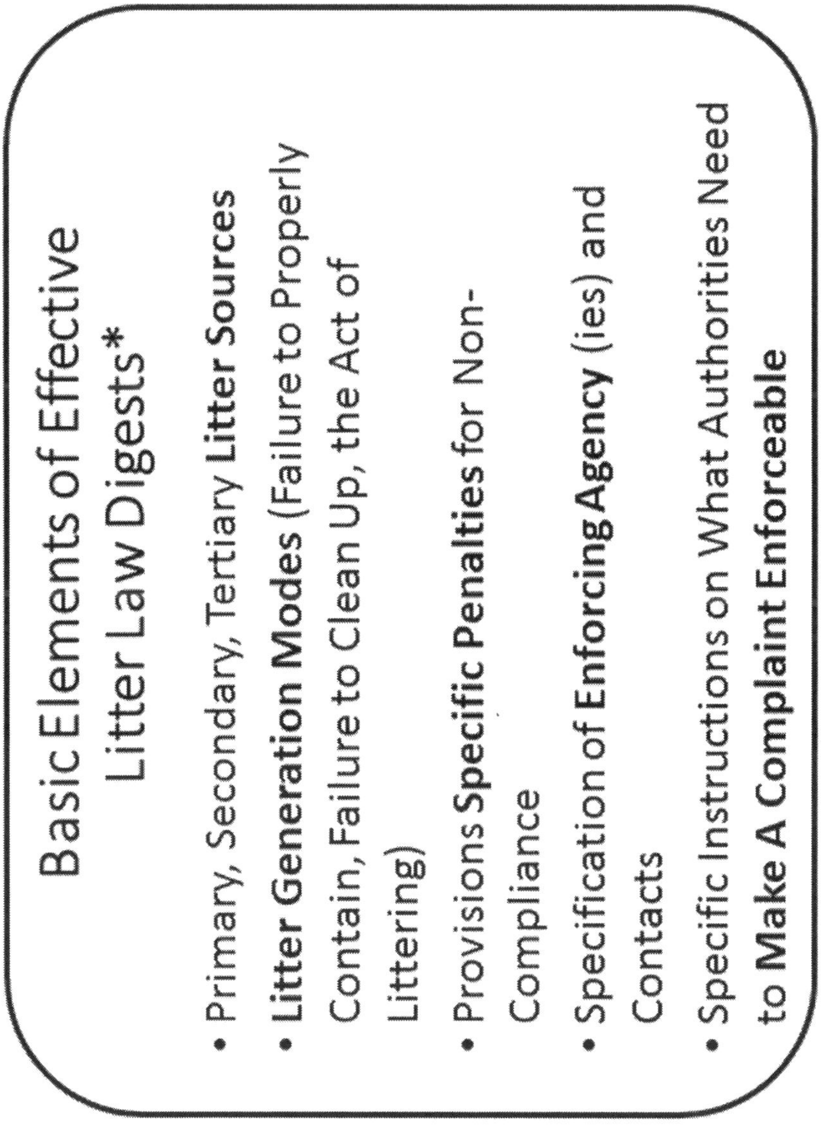

Basic Elements of Effective Litter Law Digests*

- Primary, Secondary, Tertiary **Litter Sources**
- **Litter Generation Modes** (Failure to Properly Contain, Failure to Clean Up, the Act of Littering)
- Provisions **Specific Penalties** for Non-Compliance
- Specification of **Enforcing Agency** (ies) and Contacts
- Specific Instructions on What Authorities Need to **Make A Complaint Enforceable**

Figure 19

Chapter 20
How Does Social Media Fit Into the Overall Program Communications Effort?

There was a time when many Americans were still what might be called "amedial." They lived each day with little or even no media contact. Such individuals did not interact with print or electronic media, digital social networks, or sometimes even have phone service much less smart phones. Today, however, most people have TV in their homes (though our 97.4% of all homes with TV's in America is actually only 23rd in the world!) And TV is still the most preferred way for adults to get their news. Pew Research's 2012 "Where People Got Their News Yesterday" found:

- 55% of adults got their news yesterday by watching news on TV.
- 39% of adults got their news yesterday from an online or mobile source.
- 33% of adults got their news yesterday by listening to a radio
- 29% of adults got their news yesterday by reading a newspaper (down from 55% in 1991.)

However, 39% of people got their news yesterday via some online or mobile means...up from just 24% in 2006. The big picture is that social networking and social marketing should be key elements in our overall communication planning. They should be treated as any other communications options and are subject to classic media planning and impact analysis.

Sites such as Hootsuite, "the #1 social relationships platform" according to Hootsuite, and Nimble, the world's first Intelligent Relationship platform, according to Nimble, offer multiple social networking plans, including bare bones, free options. They suggest that developing a systematic social media plan looks much like a systematic approach to any traditionally structured communications plan. The basic steps they recommend include:

Step 1: Create specific social media objectives (What are we trying to accomplish?)

Step 2: Conduct a current social media utilization audit. (What results are we already getting?)

Step 3: Create or improve your social media accounts. (Do we really need added/different social media or something else?)

Step 4: Get social media inspiration from industry leaders, competitors, if any, and clients. (Be situationally aware!)

Step 5: Create a content plan and editorials calendar. (Plan ahead!)

Step 6: Test, evaluate and adjust your social media marketing plan. (Don't assume; be accountable!)

Step 7: Author's note...we should consider applying these six steps to all of our messaging channels, including special promotion materials.

We can learn more about Hootsuite at its website, http://blog.hootsuite.com/how-to-create-a-social-media-marketing-plan, and Nimble at www.nimble.com. (No, sorry to share, this is not a paid advertisement!) We can also Google "social media marketing planning" and get over 59 million hits. A rich supply of information is online! Another excellent site can be found at https://blog.bufferapp.com/social-media-marketing-plan.

Youth communications habits are much more volatile than are those of adults. To help stay current, we can research via Google periodically, being sure to go more often to specific research sites as, at this writing, Pew Research, awber.com and clickz.com

Beware! Others' declarations that begin with "Young people these days..." "My grandchildren..." "My children/daughter(s)/son(s)..." are likely to provide us with information that will NOT be very helpful. As we consider our communications plan content, we need to identify objective, cross-sectional data, not personal war stories. Listening politely is OK; using that input to plan, probably not.

NOTES:

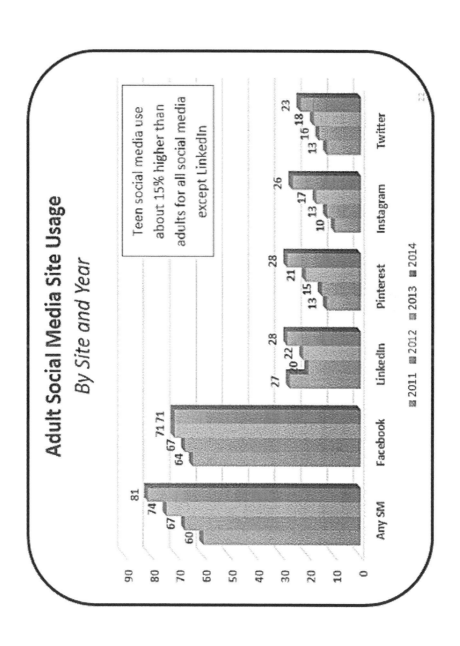

Figure 20

Chapter 21
Is There a Tool or Method to Help Keep Our Program On Mission?

Yes, there is. It addresses one of the most vexing challenges in all training, including that of KAB System training. The challenge is getting students to put into regular use back home the most critical lessons that they learn at workshops, on line, etc.

To help in this regard, this author's S.O.S. group, has developed the "Mission Keeper Form." It is a one-page checklist that is easily used by local program board and staff. Its purpose is to help affiliates make it a norm to consciously adhere to a systematic, behavior based approach when evaluating their existing projects or discussing the adoption of new programs and activities.

The top of the Mission Keeper Form is traditional and includes:

- The name of the project,
- The name of the person heading it up,
- Its start date and intended end date,
- Its budget and proposed resources to meet its costs, etc.

The bottom of the form, however, is geared specifically to the KAB System way of bringing about community wide culture change. In this area, it asks for four kinds of project information:

1. On what major decision points will the project focus? (Column A)
2. Which behavioral change strategies will be utilized? (Column B)
3. On which community sector/s will the project focus? (Column C)
4. How will a baseline and final estimations of impact be objectively measured, reported and celebrated (Column D)?

Committing to the regular use of this form will help keep programs focused on activities that have lasting impacts instead of just being done because they have always been done or just because board members think they are fun. Nothing against having fun, but let's focus when we can on leading for change that lasts!

NOTES:

KAB CULTURE CHANGE SYSTEM
MISSION KEEPER PROPOSAL AND EVALUATION FORM - PART A

KEEP _____ BEAUTIFUL, DATE: _____

			APPROVED By & Date
Proposed Title:			
Problem Or Opportunity Statement: ①			
Proposed Chair/Project Leader: ②			
Proposed Budget: ③			
Proposed Funding Resource: ④			
Proposed "Work Through Partner/s" ⑤			
Proposed Timeline ⑥	Start:	Go/No Go:	Finish:
Notes:			

1. Focusing on a specific problem or opportunity contributes to the overall project success.
2. It is generally best for the affiliate program director to be in a supporting role on a given project.
3. Include money, manpower, materials, technology, information, authority and time in your budget! (see Timeline)
4. The SOURCE or sources of each needed budget resource should be specified. Assuming the availability of assets can cause problems.
5. Few projects need to be done "solo" and working THROUGH other organizations builds capacity, strengthens bonds, and helps to change.
6. A proposed timeline helps keep all involved on mission and engaged with meeting goals.

Figure 21.1

KAB CULTURE CHANGE SYSTEM
MISSION KEEPER PROPOSAL AND EVALUATION FORM - PART B

KEEP _____ BEAUTIFUL, DATE: _____

A. Key Decision Points Focus ⑦	B. Get the Facts Focus ⑧	C. Community Sector Focus ⑨	D. Baseline, Impacts, Celebration ⑩
Business Putouts	Written Expectations	Business	Baseline
Single Family Residential Putouts			
Multi-Family Putouts	Existing Technology	Government	Mid-Stream Measurement(s)
Construction/Demolition Sites			
Loading/Receiving Areas	Current $$$ Incentives	Schools/Youth	Final Measurement
Uncovered Vehicles/Unsecured Loads			
Motorists/Boaters/Bikers	Present Reinforcement	Civic Groups	
Pedestrians/Hikers/Picnickers, etc.			
Public Gathering Places	On-Going Education	Media/PR	Celebrate!
Illegal Dumping			

Notes:

7. Greater project or program focus on one or two targeted community sub-segments, the more likely it is to bring lasting change.
8. Getting the specific facts noted here increases the likelihood of bringing about lasting change for the better. And, Education is the most
9. Projects placed "on the plate" of a specific committee gain from clearly being a part of that committee's stated goals and objectives.
10. All gains should be measurable. The very acts of setting goals, taking measurement and reporting results adds urgency and "Better" is

Figure 21.2

KAB CULTURE CHANGE SYSTEM

MISSION KEEPER PROPOSAL AND EVALUATION FORM

KEEP _____ BEAUTIFUL, DATE: _____

Proposed Title:
Proposed Problem Or Opportunity Statement: ①
Proposed Chair/Project Leader: ②
Proposed Budget: ③
Proposed Funding Resource: ④
Proposed "Work Through Partner/s" ⑤
Proposed Timeline ⑥

	A. Key Decision Points Focus ⑦	B. Get the Facts Focus ⑧	C. Community Sector Focus ⑨	D. Baseline, Impacts, Celebration ⑩
Start:			Go/No Go:	Finish:
Business Putouts		Written Expectations	Business	Baseline
Single Family Residential Putouts				
Multi-Family Putouts		Existing Technology	Government	Mid-Stream Measurement(s)
Construction/Demolition Sites				
Loading/Receiving Areas		Current $$$ Incentives	Schools/Youth	Final Measurement
Uncovered Vehicles/Unsecured Loads				
Motorists/Boaters/Bikers		Present Reinforcement	Civic Groups	
Pedestrians/Hikers/Picnickers, etc.				
Public Gathering Places		On-Going Education	Media/PR	Celebrate!
Illegal Dumping				

APPROVED
By &
Date

Notes:

1. Focusing on a specific problem or opportunity contributes to the overall project success.
2. It is generally best for the affiliate program director to be in a supporting role on any given project.
3. Include monies, manpower, materials, technology, information, authority and time in your budget (see Timeline)
4. The SOURCE or sources of each needed budget resource should be specified. Assuming the availability of assets can cause problems.
5. Few projects need to be done "solo" and working THROUGH other organizations builds capacity, strengthens bonds, and helps to change
6. A proposed timeline helps keep all involved on mission and engaged with meeting goals.
7. Greater project or program focus on one or two targeted community sub-segments, the more likely it is to bring lasting change
8. Getting the specific facts noted here increases the likelihood of bringing about lasting change for the better. And, Education is the most
9. Projects placed "on the plate" of a specific committee gain from clearly being a part of that committee's stated goals and objectives.
10. All gains should be measurable. The very acts of setting goals, taking measurement and reporting results adds urgency and "better" is

©Copyright 2014 Robert S. Horton with Sustainable Opportunities and Solutions, Inc. All rights reserved

Chapter 22
How Do We Assess New Information and Integrate It into Our Program and Behavior Management Model?

The good news is that the world of community development has changed a great deal and largely for the better since 1976. That was the year that Keep America Beautiful began rolling out what we now call the KAB System. There are dozens if not hundreds of opportunities at any given time to attend workshops on recycling, beautification, watershed management, trash free waters, community-based marketing, and many other related issues.

However, few if any of these programs have the KAB Systems' 40-year plus validating experience in the field with over 600 communities across the U.S. Unlike other programs, the KAB System can be and is led by paid and volunteer staff that do not require extensive training or education beyond that which KAB and its state leaders offer. And the KAB System's theoretical provenance is golden. It is largely based on Kurt Lewin's widely recognized and very practical Unfreeze-Change-Refreeze and Force Field theories. As KAB's consultant, Dr. Wes Schulz put it at the 2015 Annual Conference, "the KAB System is solid." (See Chapter 29.)

There is an increasing amount of information available, but little of it thus far is specifically oriented to the KAB System, even some of that which is offered at KAB's own conferences. Hence, it falls to each individual coordinator to make his or her own decisions about making the best use of information that comes in each speech, workshop, webinar or other presentation they attend.

The first decision is deciding whether to set aside their existing behavior-based KAB System and adopt some other overall approach. As even the most interesting new programs are not as comprehensive, systematic or well-proven as our KAB System, we should seriously hesitate before going some new route.

Alternately, we can commit to doing "planned listening" that helps us listen for selected information we could best use to augment and strengthen our existing program.

As we think of improving rather than replacing our existing programs, here are some basic questions we can ask ourselves as we learn along the way:

1. Does this presentation offer useful ideas for attracting added community leadership support for our program?
2. Does this presentation suggest useful ideas for updating our written expectations about waste handling/waste diversion-recycling/beautification?
3. Does this presentation offer useful ideas about new helping technology or information that makes complying with our written expectations easier or more affordable?
4. Does this presentation provide insights into useful economic or non-economic incentives for encouraging compliance with written ordinances, or negative incentives that discourage non-compliance?
5. Does this presentation suggest useful ideas for strengthening our enforcement efforts and/or making our existing enforcement more visible and tangible?
6. Does this presentation suggest new, useful ideas for improving or expanding our educational programming?
7. Did this speaker/presenter do a good job of relating his or her ideas and material to our KAB System principles?
8. Did I receive both interesting as well as useful information that was not necessarily KAB System relevant?
9. Finally, did we ask our national or state program staff to please give future presenters basic KABS information and request that they make their presentations as KABS relevant as possible?

A presentation/presenter rating form is provided to help us make the most of this systematic rating process.

NOTES:

KAB System-Based Presentation Evaluation Form
5 = Highest/Most Useful Rating, 1 = Lowest

Presentation Name _____ Date _____

1.	Suggests new, useful ideas for attracting community leadership support	5	4	3	2	1
2.	Suggests new, useful ideas for updating waste handling ordinances	5	4	3	2	1
3.	Suggests new, useful ideas for compliance enhancing technology or information	5	4	3	2	1
4.	Suggests new, useful ideas for clarifying economic impacts of compliance and non-compliance with ordinances	5	4	3	2	1
5.	Suggests new, useful ideas for improving or expanding our educational programming	5	4	3	2	1
6.	Suggests new, useful ideas for strengthening our enforcement and/or making more of the enforcement we already have	5	4	3	2	1
7.	This speaker/presenter seemed to be well-grounded in the KAB System principles	5	4	3	2	1
8.	Useful or interesting information though not KAB System relevant	5	4	3	2	1
9.	I need to ask KAB or whomever to ask speakers to read a KAB System overview before presenting	5	4	3	2	1

NOTES:

Figure 22

Chapter 23
What Is a Mantra and How Can It Help Us?

Good change management can be compared to teaching new plays to a ball team. Simplicity and repetition are paramount. The slogan-like phrases we emphasis must be easy to remember and strategies easy to use in times of chaotic change. (P.S. - ALL change is chaotic!). They are the proven, basic action steps toward solutions when specific solution-oriented steps have not yet become routine. Simple phrases become slogans that keep us focused. Some that can serve us especially well as we adopt and seek to strengthen commitments to the KAB System include:

A. **Work THROUGH Existing Organizations!** KABS program managers typically face significant educational leverage challenges. The average KABS affiliate has about 140,000 residents being served by one or two staff and a handful of volunteers. Perhaps 13 volunteers with a modest budget and those few staffers are tasked with changing the minds and altering the behavior of all their people; youth, adults and seniors. The leverage ratio is 1,000 to one! So, they MUST recruit and train a large number of "middlemen" or "wholesalers" to carry the message. Working through existing organizations helps level the playing field and make their job more doable.

B. **Sponsor change management *WORKSHOPS!*** If all a program committee did was to hold setting-specific workshops for educational, recreational, residential, communications, governmental, communications, and workplace sector audiences, chances are that their community would get cleaner and stay cleaner quickly. Teaching others to manage change is like raising children. It is imperative that we stop trying to think for, decide for, and clean up after others. We must focus on teaching and empowering them to make their own better tomorrows happen.

C. Commit to Being Accountable starting on Day One!

Being accountable means taking rational "before action baselines" and then measuring and reporting real changes in ambient litter levels, recycling levels, and/or beautification. ALL other measures and stats are secondary!

D. Include, Don't Exclude!

E. Work the System. In Order. Completely. Every time.

F. Celebrate!

NOTES:

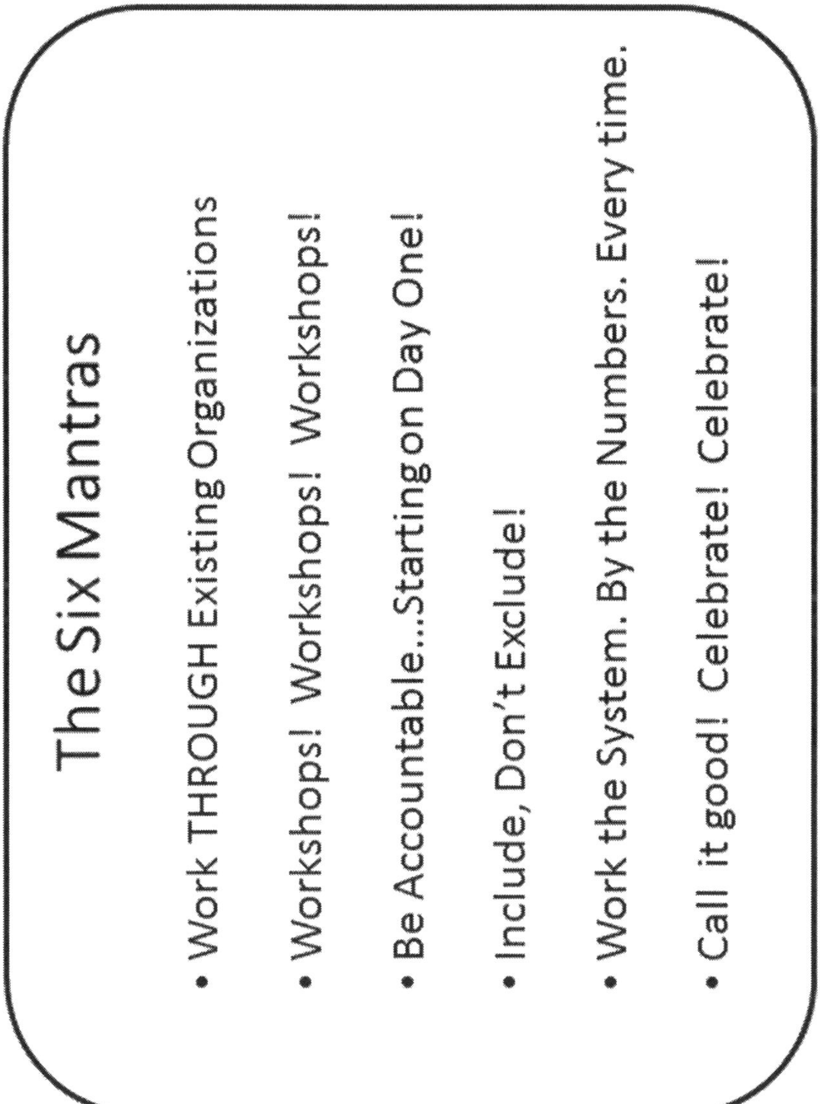

The Six Mantras

• Work THROUGH Existing Organizations

• Workshops! Workshops! Workshops!

• Be Accountable...Starting on Day One!

• Include, Don't Exclude!

• Work the System. By the Numbers. Every time.

• Call it good! Celebrate! Celebrate!

Figure 23

Supplemental Questions

Chapter 24
Our City Management Maintains That They Do Not Have Enough Money to Help Fund Our Program. Are They Really Saving Money?

Probably not. One fast way to get our point across regarding real savings is to compare what it costs our city (taxpayers) to collect one ton of waste at curbside vs. the costs to Streets or Parks to collect one ton of litter. The difference can be persuasively large. One affiliate did a quick analysis in recent years and found that curbside trash collection cost Solid Waste about $160 per ton or 8 cents per pound. By comparison, their Streets Department spent $1,600 per ton or 80 cents per pound collecting loose litter and debris.

The high cost of failing to minimize littering by educating the public to properly contain their trash was very high indeed in that city! In this example, that differential cost was 72 cents per pound for hundreds of tons of litter per year. It finally cost the public and private sectors an estimated extra $8 million and more annually.

In another city, a commercial developer who had flown in a large international investor discovered the high cost of litter and weeds the hard way. Half way to his office from the airport, the European investor asked him how soon he could catch a flight back home. Flustered, the developer asked him why. The investor pointed out the window and said, "Yours is a new and successful city, yet all I see along your freeways are tall weeds and litter that looks to have been mowed by uncaring crews. If you are so bold as to allow your poor management of your front door to go unaddressed, I cannot imagine what kind of short cuts you may take in managing my investment after I leave town. Just take me back to the airport and I will find my way home!" The developer was unable to overcome the investor's first impression and had to find other, less favorable financing elsewhere.

Our city may very well reduce outgoing cash flow in the short term by postponing our program or providing fewer support dollars than we have requested. And they may call that "saving money."

Nevertheless, studies of the high and often hidden costs of doing too little litter abatement are well documented. Their "savings" may very well not be savings at all.

Research by KAB and selected affiliates, coupled with mild inflation, indicates that the simple act of cleaning up community litter in 2016 may be costing upwards of $45.00 per capita per year. If Ourtown has a population of 100,000 residents, that adds up to over $4,500,000 per year. Against that expense estimate, our request for $45,000 (1% of the cost of litter) to add a Community Educator to help people better contain their trash and prevent litter starts to look much more reasonable.

We can help attract more funds by better defining the problem, beginning with gathering new litter cost data. Using the Litter Cost Information Gathering Form at the end of this chapter can help us do that readily. With the support of the city manager (highly recommended), we can start by helping the city see how much it is spending cleaning up loose trash. Often, cities do not know their litter costs because litter clean-up expense is spread across multiple departments and not individually coded in their chart of accounts. Streets, storm water, public health, courts, parks, public works, and others may well have separate budgets. We can facilitate a survey that surfaces those expenditures and brings them to light as a cumulative total.

We can also do similar studies with retailers such as shopping centers, with neighborhood associations, with multi-family communities (apartments), with school systems, and at larger workplaces.

A "sampling approach" can be taken without doing a "scientific sample," much less asking every member of a group to respond.

For example, if building codes tells us there are 45 motel/hotel properties in town, we can go to just 5-10 of them, from top notch to marginal and ask them to complete our form as well as they can. When they are done, we can share something like:

"While our survey of 8 motels and hotels in town does not represent a scientific sample, we can say that we asked hotel/motel class A, B, and C property managers to respond. Their

input indicates that Class A properties are spending over $1,600 per unit annually to pick up litter from their properties, their parking lots, and the common areas along the roads that border their properties. Class B properties are spending about $1,200 per unit annually and Class C properties are spending about $800 per unit annually. If all 15 Class A, B and C properties, each with an average of 100 units, are experiencing similar expenses, it is fair to estimate that our hotel/motel sector alone is spending well over $5,000,000 a year picking up loose trash and helping to keep its first appearances as positive as possible.

This can be done in virtually every sector desired. Every survey outcome completed adds to the argument that less prevention is not a wise move for the public or the private sectors. There really is a surprisingly high cost attendant to doing too little litter prevention.

In fact, as high as results of this calculation of litter costs may appear, they pale in comparison to the costs not computed including those associated with broken windshields (flying rock damage), equipment damage/loss, fires in rubbish and grass, highway injuries/deaths (from striking-swerving around roadbed litter), inventory shrinkage - lost product. litter removal crew injuries/deaths, lost residential/commercial sales/leases/rents, not maximizing aluminum, corrugated, glass, paper, plastic recycling, increased water purification expense, possible white goods deaths (locked doors), wildlife damage/loss, and worksite injuries & workmen's comp premiums

NOTES:

SAMPLE LITTER COST INFORMATION GATHERING FORM

ORGANIZATION NAME: _____

1. Please use this form to estimate the hours and dollars that you, your supervisors, your staff, your contract laborers, etc. spend on litter pickup. Your estimate may be on a weekly, monthly or annual basis.

Labor Type	Hours	Rates	Frequency Dy/Wk/Mon	Totals
Supervisory				$
Straight Time				$
Overtime				$
Subtotal				$
Benefits/Insur.				
Contract Labor				$
Temp Labor				$
Community Service		$15-$30		$
Volunteers		**$23.07**		$
Totals	0	n/a	n/a	$
Materials				$
Equipment and Depreciation				$
Grand Total Annual Expense				$

*** The value of community service and volunteer hours depends on usual costs or fines forgiven for such work.

2. Are there improvements in ordinances or changes in enforcement practices that would help you in your work? You may submit these suggestions separately and anonymously.

Estimating the High Cost of Doing Too Little Litter Prevention

Figure 24

Chapter 25
How Can We Make Room on Our Board for Fresh Thinking and New Energy Without Alienating Our Long-Serving Members...Many of Them Founders?

Nobody wants to hurt the feelings of a long-serving volunteer who must be asked to step aside. Understandably, many ways to deal with this question have been tried

1. We can pass a change to our bylaws to allow more seats on the board. This avoids removing the subject board member or members but dilutes their impact with more, new votes.
2. We can invoke the existing provisions in our bylaws that state that there are term limits for board members and officers.
3. Don't have such a provision? Ask around for others' wording, or ask your lawyer to help you, then market the language needed to increase board size or limit terms.

Tried all those to no avail? I hear you. Many of us have been in those places, tried those things, but not succeeded. Another and hopefully less drama-filled option is #4.

4. Create, revitalize, or redefine a "Friends of Keep Ourtown Beautiful" advisory group. The keys to the success of this group are those of recruiting a strong but non-controlling leader and regularly giving this group the chance to consider and make recommendations on items of substance. Asking your outgoing (or now outgoing) Board President to head up this group may be a useful tactic for you. If not, consider asking a prior board member.

Hallmarks of a Friends group can be:

- Infrequent meetings, for instance quarterly.
- Be open to including past/outgoing board members and key volunteers as well as key community leaders who have never

been your volunteers or board members such as elected officials, past Chamber presidents, etc.

- Urge attendance but make it optional.
- Provide a defined but "open" agenda to encourage the free flow of ideas.
- Work to recruit community "big dogs" that have both strong records of accomplishment and access to resources.
- See that Friends group members receive specific feedback on the progress of recommendations that they have made.
- Seek new members with "outside perspectives" to add to rather than simply repeat or coattail known positions.
- Definitely provide some kind of brief orientation for new Friends that highlights the key steps of the KAB System including the five behavior change strategies we use to get our measureable results.
- Include some kind of recognition such as breakfast, lapel pins, name badges, awards, mayoral thank you letters, a seat on the July 4th Parade float, etc. that offers the trappings of privilege at minimal out-of-pocket cost.

NOTES:

SAMPLE BY-LAW LANGUAGE AUTHORIZING AND CREATING AN ADVISORY BOARD OR "FRIENDS OF KEEP OURTOWN BEAUTIFUL GROUP"

ARTICLE XI. ADVISORY BOARD

The Keep Ourtown Beautiful Board shall create and maintain a KOB Advisory Board whose members shall be community leaders and spokespersons nominated by the KOB Board and its own membership, subject to approval of the KOB Board.

Advisory Board members such as business leaders, philanthropists, and elected officials may or may not have ever served on the KOB Board or as KOB volunteers. The Immediate Past President of KOB might be asked to serve as Chair of this Advisory Board unless the Advisory Board has already has such a leader.

Advisory Board purposes shall include but not be limited to:

1. Serving as a sounding board for KOB promotions and proposals.

2. Helping to develop outside funds and other non-municipal resources for KOB's programs.

3. Increasing community-wide awareness of KOB and its mission.

4. Providing advice to KOB's Board on existing physical, financial and legislative challenges.

   And Such other functions as may be designated by the KOB Board.

Figure 25

Chapter 26
What More Do We Know About Bringing About Change at the Individual Level?

Before we look at this question, it is well to remind ourselves of four things about the Keep America Beautiful System.:

1. The KABS works best where there is a tangible "sense of community" in place. Thus, affiliates tasked to serve regions, counties and large cities have special challenges.
2. The KABS focuses on indirectly changing the behavior of unidentified (and hard to identify) individuals by changing the multiple social environments in which they live.
3. The KABS has a sterling record of success in over 600 communities, stretching back to the mid-1970s.
4. Any project that we launch to bring about change at the individual level would fare best if we assure that it is working in concert with local KABS programming.

Those things noted, we might be interested in what is known as the "Stages of Change," or Trans Theoretical Model (TTM). This widely used model in the world of public health was initially based on extensive research on various methods for helping smokers stop smoking. Its first conclusion is that all methods work to some degree some of the time. Its second conclusion is that what works best is largely determined by each individual's "stage of readiness to change." Those stages are:

- Pre-Contemplation (Never)
- Contemplation (Maybe)
- Preparation (Soon)
- Action (Now)
- Maintenance (Forever/Never)

Success then is most likely when there is a good *fit* between our strategies and the *stages of readiness to change* of our individual audience members. So, does this mean that our communications job has to become five times more difficult? No, but it does help explain why some of our appeals for volunteers, for donations, and for behavior change seem to go unheeded. It can also help us to choose for our communications those tools that are best suited to our specific purposes of awareness building, of fostering change and of maintaining new best practices.

To help in the matching of tools to audiences, Prochaska and DiClemente's TTM suggests three simple assessment questions we can use to help us determine an organization's stage of readiness to change:

Q# 1: Are you seriously intending to make changes in the next 6 months? (If "No," stop here, thank them, leave your card and brochure, and move on. If "Yes," ask Questions #2 and #3.)

Q# 2: Are you planning to change in the next month?

Q# 3: Have you tried to change in the past 12 months?

Precontemplation is indicated by a "no" answer to # 1;

Contemplation by a "yes" to # 1 and "no" to either #2 or #3;

Preparation by a "yes" to # 1, #2 and #3.

Bonus: Both the TTM stages and the stage transition information below can be used by us to temper the relationship we have with community leaders. Whether we want to discuss the installation of a new affiliate program or to upgrade an existing program, it is very likely that we will first confront resistance and skepticism, then move to "maybe someday," etc. Isn't it encouraging to understand that even a flat out "No!" can be just another part of a commitment process!

To help with this process, look over the following three exhibits.

The first provides a graphic overview of Stages of Change process. The second focuses on the educational material that is suited to each stage of change. The third exhibit coaches us on the task of helping folks transition from stage to stage as needed.

We may also be interested in doing some outside reading and perhaps attending a workshop on the subject of "social marketing" or, variously, "community based social marketing." We should always be open-minded and willing to learn.

I would add that, in my graduate and post-graduate studies and since, I have never encountered another proven, large-scale program like the KAB System. It has:

- Remained community based from its inception in the mid-1970s to today.
- Worked affordably across communities of all sizes.
- Involved hundreds of thousands of local citizens at all levels annually.
- Demonstrated that an open structure system that recommends "what" must happen, leaving much of the "how" in the hands of local affiliate volunteers, works.
- Against all odds, used its natural fit and appeal to withstand the onslaught of almost four decades of "better ideas."

NOTES:

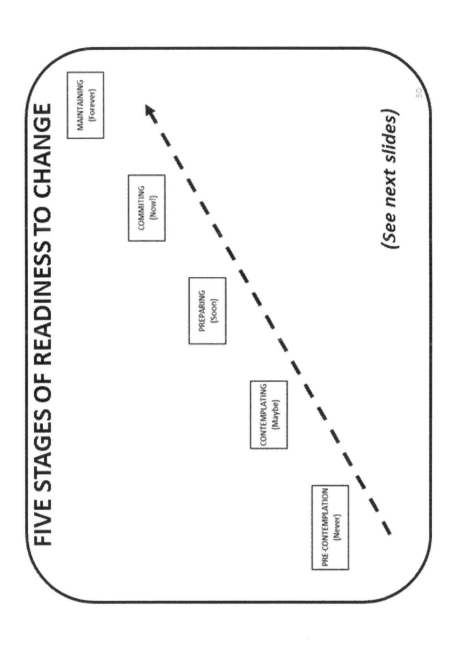

Figure 26.1

FITTING EDUCATIONAL MATERIALS TO STAGES OF READINESS TO CHANGE

Materials Supporting Precontemplative and Contemplative Stages:

Community appearance appraisals, Posters, Corporate and municipal cost audits, Payroll stuffers, Employee interest surveys, Calendars, Stages of change readiness surveys, Table tents, Newsletters, Corporate and community awareness presentations

Materials Supporting Preparation and Commitment Stages:

Self-directed publications, Formal action programs, Communicators with study guides, Self-directed programs, Online research tools, Audio tapes, Tele-support. Multimedia programs. Internet/intranet

Materials Supporting On-Going Maintenance Stage

Targeted newsletter/s, Tele-support, Booster classes, Posters, Payroll stuffers

(See next slide)

Figure 26.2

Helping Small Resident Groups*
Move from Stage to Stage

Transition Support Strategies

Precontemplation To Contemplation	Contemplation To Preparation	Preparation To Action	Action To Maintenance
Emphasize Benefits High Information/ Low Pressure	Address Change Discomforts Focus on Small Thinking Changes -> Big Action Changes	Setting of Action Dates Action Oriented Programs Maintain Realistic Expectations Quietly Expect 3 or 4 Cycles	Help Strategize to Prevent Temporary Relapses Anchor Benefits -> Long-Term Benefits

* Or occasionally key individuals

Figure 26.3

153

Chapter 27
Are Our Prior Year KAB and State Office Activity Reports of Any Practical Use?

Absolutely! Completing our annual and semi-annual reports to Keep America Beautiful and/or our state office is a smart business practice in any case. The timely completion of these reports gives us current information about the state of our programs as compared with our previous years of operation and with standardized state and national program norms. It can also definitely improve our chances of getting all the recognition our volunteers richly deserve and grant funds that our programs richly need.

Rewards and recognition can have a hidden benefit as administrative policy out-of-city and out-of-state travel blocks often disappear when community recognition is to be received.

Unfortunately, low production years due to board or staff turnover, funding and budget shortfalls, etc. can make an affiliate program feel more vulnerable to staffing or budget cuts. Even high production years can yield increased vulnerability, as expectations of that level of performance become "the new normal."

The key presenting weakness for ongoing programs is that of being reviewed just one year at a time.

A great defense to turn this apparent weakness into a strength is to begin presenting each year's performance as part of a moving cluster of up to five years at a time.

As can be seen in this example from Keep Irving (Tx) Beautiful's "5 Year Good News Performance Report," the lowest public benefit noted is $255,000 and the highest almost $400,000. However, added together with the other three years in this report, the total public benefit exceeds $1,500,000.

This documenting of productive programming, coupled with measured reductions in community litter levels, provides both a defensive and an offensive tool to this affiliate:

- If suggestions are made to reduce or eradicate the $144,000 budget of our program, we can point to the $1.5 Million in benefits. Few city departments offer a cost-benefit ratio equal to ours, much less $3.38 in benefits to the community for each dollar invested. For the record, that cost-benefit ratio is modest compared to those of some other affiliates.
- If suggestions are made to increase formal expectations of the program without commensurate budgetary support, the gradual trend forward can be cited, helping to temper unrealistic predictions.
- When seeking additional public or community funding, this program presentation can point to a high level of benefits, its recurring cost-benefit ratio, and its well-documented total benefit to residents and taxpayers.
- Finally, the backside of this one page cost-benefit review is an ideal position for noting awards of recognition received over the same five-year periods and performance statistics such the audiences to whom presentations have been made, events participated in by name, etc.

Full-size, color copies of all materials shown in this handbook are available by contacting the author.

NOTES:

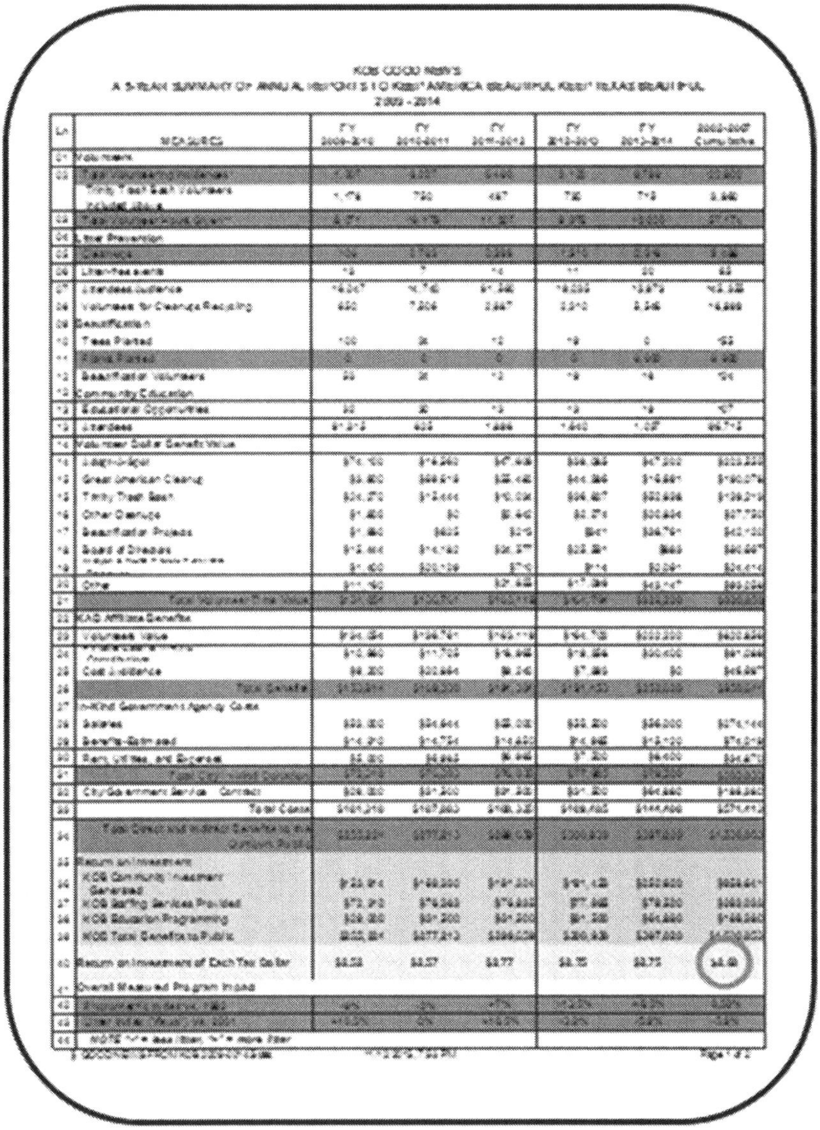

Figure 27.1

KEEP OURTOWN BEAUTIFUL
A 5-YEAR SUMMARY OF AWARDS AND RECOGNITION RECEIVED
2009 To 2014

#							
01	KTB President's Circle Award	***	***	***	***	***	
02	KTB President's Circle Recognition Group		****	****	****	****	
03	KAB Innovation Award		****			****	
04	KTB Gold Star Affiliate Recognition		****	****	****	****	
05	Award for Excellence to KOB/City of		****	****		****	
06	Representation on KTB Board of Directors				****	****	
07	KTB Ebby Halliday and Maurice Acers Business and Industry Award – Second Place Waste Management, Inc.					****	
08	KTB Ebby Halliday and Maurice Acers Business and Industry Award Certificate of Merit B&E Systems-Ourtown					****	
09	KTB Ebby Halliday and Maurice Acers Business and Industry Award Certificate of Merit Ocean USA-Ourtown					****	
10	KTB Ebby Halliday and Maurice Acers Business and Industry Award Honorable Mention Law College Association					****	
11	KTB Ebby Halliday/Maurice Acers Business Honorable Mention-Ebby Halliday/SBC	****					
12	KTB Ebby Halliday/Maurice Acers Business Certificate of Merit Williams Towers Recycling Program			****			
13	KTB Government Award/Honorable Mention-Ourtown B&E's Inspch'n			****			
14	KTB Certificate of Merit Ourtown Rambler					****	
15	KTB Portho Jackson Youth Leadership Award Certificate of Merit T.J. Lee Elementary Lion's Pride Green Team					****	
16	KTB Portho Jackson Youth Leadership Certificate of Merit M.O. Lively Elementary					****	
17	KTB Portho Jackson Youth Leadership Honorable Mention Alpha Zeta Eta Chapter of Phi Theta Kappa Honor Society					****	
18	KTB Portho Jackson Youth Leadership Honorable Mention-Naming Jr Historians	****					
19	KTB Sadie Ray Graff Education Certificate of Merit J.O. Davis Elementary Re-entification Committee					****	
20	KTB Sadie Ray Graff Education Certificate of Merit John W. and Margie Stiper					****	
21	KTB Sadie Ray Graff Elementary Third Place Award Otis Brown Elementary			****			
22	KTB Sadie Ray Graff Second Place School District Award Ourtown ISD & Partners Green Team Program			****			
23	North Texas Corporate Recycling Alliance, 2012 Recycling Partnership Award of Excellence Ourtown ISD & Partners Green Team			****			

* Some duplication results from individual volunteers serving in more than one capacity or event.
**2010-2011 range is result of highly successful Business Committee "Clic on Your Files Day" program
***Yet cost-benefit research: minimum areas used for non-board volunteer time value.

Figure 27.2

158

Chapter 28
Can We See the Normative System Culture Change Process That Underpins Our KAB System?

Of course. Looking at Dr. Robert Allen's Normative System Culture Change Process diagram, we see that it is both sequential and systematic. And we can readily see its similarity to our own Get the Facts, Involve ALL the People, Plan Systematically, Focus on Results and Provide Positive Reinforcement.

Like our own KAB System variation, Dr. Allen's NSCCP actually operates in a circular fashion, Those who use either system often progress two or even three steps forward, then one step back before moving forward once again."

Do note that while Dr. Allen's program design contains similarities to our own KAB System, it does NOT note the specific behavioral change strategies that make to our solid waste handling system so unique. That said, there are key features of Allen's original model that were very much parts of our original KAB System. These bear renewed emphasis at the local level and include doing system (program) introductions through introductory briefing presentations and community system integration through onsite training workshops.

Re-energizing those vital elements can be done and should be at the local level, regardless of what may be happening at the state or local levels. Based largely on Dr. Allen's specific recommendations in the mid-1970s, steps toward accomplishing this revitalization include:

1. Minimizing the launching or continued operation of programs or projects that lack substantial leadership commitment. (Use the Mission Keeper Form.)
2. Recommit to working primarily *through* existing organizations that have both their leaders' and their middle

managers' commitment in place. The word "through" deserves its emphasis here. It is not "with" or "with the support of," but "*through*," connoting their full commitment to community improvement through their commitment to self-improvement first.

3. Minimize applause-as-results presentations and laser-focus instead on presentations that lead to community organizations such as major employers, business associations, civic organizations, churches, school systems or whole campuses, and government agencies committing to attend our workshops and engage with our programs.

4. Use those workshops to teach participants how to integrate the KAB System of updating written expectations, etc. into the best practices and routines of their workplaces, learning places and so on.

Beyond this diagram, Dr. Allen and his team characterized what was not working:

Cleanups: They are reactive, failing to directly address the underlying problem of littering and its normative cultural system of support and permissiveness.

Narrow Appeals: Programs relying on minimal support of, for example, scouts, churches, or even cities are unlikely to become sustainable, community-wide culture changing movements.

Annual Projects: They do not deal with the daily, year-round nature of litter generation.

Problem Focused Appeals: We need people to engage fully with solution-based activities, not problems.

NOTES:

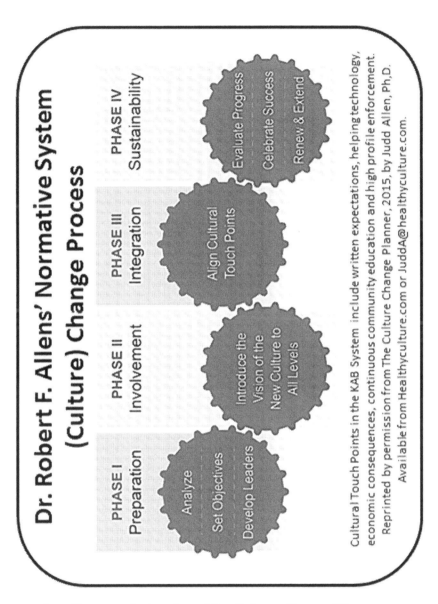

Reprinted by permission from The Culture Change Planner, 2015, by Judd Allen, Ph.D. Available from Healthyculture.com or JuddA@healthyculture.com.

Figure 28

Chapter 29
What Is This "Promise of the KAB System" That I Hear About From Time to Time?

The Promise of the KAB System is that it can be adapted to serve almost any field where lasting change for the better hinges on systematically and affordably bringing about sustainable human behavior change. Almost 40 years of successful practice in the field affirm its effectiveness. This achievement can be said to largely rest on its classic three-legged stool of support.

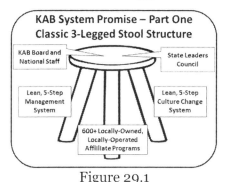

Figure 29.1

This deceptively simple model, strengthened by regular reporting, numerous awards and recognition opportunities annually, and occasional grants has proven sturdy and successful.

The KAB System as we know and practice it is an outgrowth of the wisdom of two social psychologists: Dr. Kurt Lewin, known as "the father of social psychology," and Dr. Robert Francis Allen, an early leader in the field of public and private sector wellness promotion.

Allen was surely Dr. Lewin's most ardent and prolific student as he fathered the KAB System. Both men believed that groups of people could work together with the proper plans and achieve better tomorrows.

Among his numerous practical theories, Dr. Lewin introduced his Unfreeze-Change-Refreeze theory. Unfreeze Refreeze or UCR, tells us to analyze, make changes and restore stability. Lewin used the example of melting a block of ice, dealing with the resulting water, and refreezing the water in a different shape to conclude.

We can imagine, for example, steps needed to melt several cubes of ice from our refrigerator icemaker, containing the melted ice in a pitcher, adding some cake coloring and then pouring the colored water into moon, star and sun shaped forms as part of a birthday celebration for a child. Unfreeze, Change, Refreeze; a good analogy for explaining needed changes and benefits of change to others.

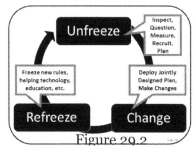

Figure 29.2

Lewin also cautioned that simplistic changes that did not encompass all the forces supporting and resisting movement to a new level or place could mislead us to thinking that we had accomplished lasting change but only creating activity and chaos.

He called the theory that he formulated to deal with multiple opposing variables "Force Field Theory."

This theory, applied to our work, reminds us that we cannot just change enforcement norms but must also change written expectations, technology, benefits and penalties, and public education norms in order to achieve and sustain the clean community goals that we have adopted.

Perhaps Lewin's most famous quote is "There is nothing quite so practical as a theory that works." And so it is as his thinking is integrated in current management philosophies and strategies such as "community based social marketing."

CBSM identifies the positive and negative forces of Lewin's Force Field Theory as "barriers and benefits." New labels, similar principles.

Dr. Robert Francis Allen, a Ph.D. in social psychology and political science, furthered Lewin's work. He blended it with other recognized psychological thinking and created his Normative System Change Process. A simplified version of his field-tested model is what we today call the Keep America Beautiful System or KAB System (KABS).

Allen's KAB System model integrates Lewin's proven collective behavior change theory with modern management practices. This means that when we "Get the Facts" we must get them about the nature and scope of litter in general and then, locally, about pertinent written expectation such as ordinances, about compliance facilitating technology such as litter receptacles and car litter bags, about the consequences, economic and otherwise of complying and not complying with the written  Dr. Robert F. Allen expectations, about publicity surrounding enforcement practices and finally about year-round, community-wide education that teaches people about the first 4 behavior influencing strategies.

The promise of what we learn when we fully master the KAB System is that it can be applied in virtually any setting where human behavior needs to be altered in large numbers. Recycling, beautifying, energy conserving, water conserving, air quality maintaining, and so many other human behavior patterns can be improved with its help and comparatively few resources.

As Margaret Mead put it, "Never doubt that a small group of thoughtful, committed citizens can change the world; indeed, it's the only thing that ever has."

In the exhibit for this chapter, you will find a one-page flow chart that depicts a blend of Dr. Allen's Normative System Culture Change Process in its Keep America Beautiful System configuration that incorporates Dr. Lewin's Unfreeze-Change-Re-Freeze and Force Field Theory as well as Drs. Prochaska and DiClemente's Stages of Change process. Just imagine if you will all that we could do with that culture change script to guide us! Imagine!

NOTES:

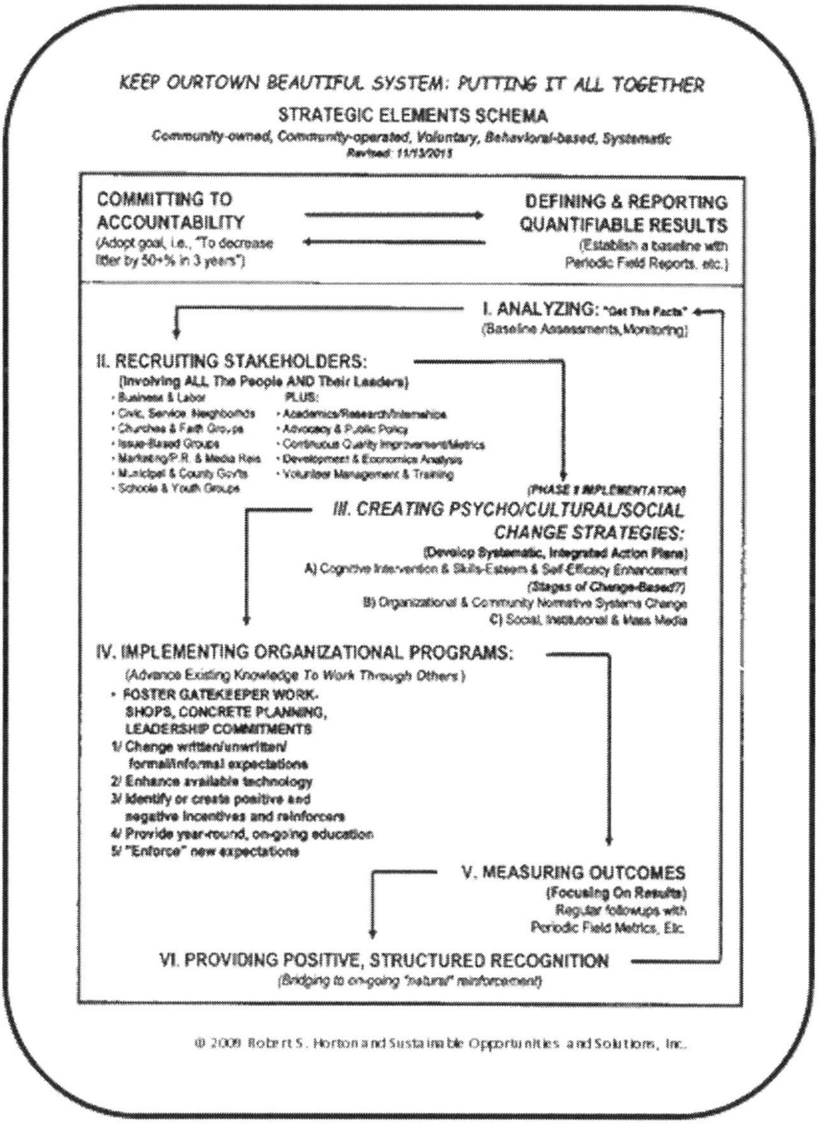

KEEP OURTOWN BEAUTIFUL SYSTEM: PUTTING IT ALL TOGETHER

STRATEGIC ELEMENTS SCHEMA

Community-owned, Community-operated, Voluntary, Behavioral-based, Systematic
Revised: 11/13/2011

COMMITTING TO ACCOUNTABILITY
(Adopt goal, i.e., "To decrease litter by 50+% in 3 years")

DEFINING & REPORTING QUANTIFIABLE RESULTS
(Establish a baseline with Periodic Field Reports, etc.)

I. ANALYZING: "Get The Facts"
(Baseline Assessments, Monitoring)

II. RECRUITING STAKEHOLDERS:
(Involving ALL The People AND Their Leaders)
- Business & Labor   PLUS:
- Civic, Service Neighborhds   · Academics/Research/Internships
- Churches & Faith Groups   · Advocacy & Public Policy
- Issue-Based Groups   · Continuous Quality Improvement/Metrics
- Marketing/P.R. & Media Reis   · Development & Economics Analysis
- Municipal & County Gov'ts   · Volunteer Management & Training
- Schools & Youth Groups

(PHASE I IMPLEMENTATION)

III. CREATING PSYCHO/CULTURAL/SOCIAL CHANGE STRATEGIES:
(Develop Systematic, Integrated Action Plans)
A) Cognitive Intervention & Skills-Esteem & Self-Efficacy Enhancement
(Stages of Change-Based?)
B) Organizational & Community Normative Systems Change
C) Social, Institutional & Mass Media

IV. IMPLEMENTING ORGANIZATIONAL PROGRAMS:
(Advance Existing Knowledge To Work Through Others)
· FOSTER GATEKEEPER WORK-SHOPS, CONCRETE PLANNING, LEADERSHIP COMMITMENTS
1/ Change written/unwritten/ formal/informal expectations
2/ Enhance available technology
3/ Identify or create positive and negative incentives and reinforcers
4/ Provide year-round, on-going education
5/ "Enforce" new expectations

V. MEASURING OUTCOMES
(Focusing On Results)
Regular followups with Periodic Field Metrics, Etc.

VI. PROVIDING POSITIVE, STRUCTURED RECOGNITION
(Bridging to on-going "natural" reinforcement)

© 2009 Robert S. Horton and Sustainable Opportunities and Solutions, Inc.

Figure 29.4

Chapter 30
Avoiding Change Program Failure Syndrome

In closing, we must be willing to learn from others and from **our** own disappointments well as our victories,

Throughout this handbook, we have seen opportunities to broaden and expand our understanding of the traditional steps of the Keep America Beautiful System. The KAB System is itself an evolution of the former Clean Community System which was an adaptation of a highly successful predecessor, the Normative System Change Process which has itself evolved to become the Normative System Culture Change Process. We have seen options to build on the KAB System by:

- Using behavioral research from the field of public health,
- Incorporating complex change management wisdom from the workplace,
- Broadening our definition of "major sources of litter,"
- Letting the four-step KABS Behavioral Management Process become a five-step process by acknowledging the economic factors that are ever at play.

We can also bring failure upon our own efforts. Dr. Robert F. Allen, our KAB System designer, was one of the most innovative and prolific corporate and community change consultants in modern history. Yet, as was noted elsewhere here, about seven in 10 of all professionally designed and launched culture change programs fail, at least in the American workplace.

Hence, Dr. Allen published, with his colleague, Stan Silverzweig, the following list of "How change programs fail", in the prestigious MIT Sloan Review. This list was based on his own extensive experiences in communities and workplaces.

How Culture Change Programs Fail

- By getting only lip-service support from management.
- By adhering to traditional "win-lose" attitudes.
- By inadequately involving of all levels of participants.
- By paying insufficient attention to mid-level leaders.
- By failing to win sufficient support of first line supervisors.
- By setting too quick a pace to the change effort.
- By adopting inappropriate levels of expectations.
- By failure to internalize (acculturate) the change process.

This is not a whimsical list. It reveals serious symptoms of program dysfunction, based on the experiences of one of America's leading culture change management experts. As professionals in our field, we are privileged to have these alerts without ourselves suffering from them. We can and must be watchful for these program deficiencies and move to cure them whenever and however we can.

On the other hand, if the maladies noted are not being addressed satisfactorily and resolved, we should consider separating ourselves in a caring and professional manner. This frees our presently served population to go its own way. Moreover, it frees us to then seek to serve another population that is better able to take advantage of our skills, values, knowledge, and perspectives. Hopefully, **Lessons** can help to further minimize this already atypical situation.

In closing, I wish you good luck, great courage, and lasting change for the better!

To thine own self be true, and it must follow, as the night the day, thou canst not then be false to any man. William Shakespeare

NOTES:

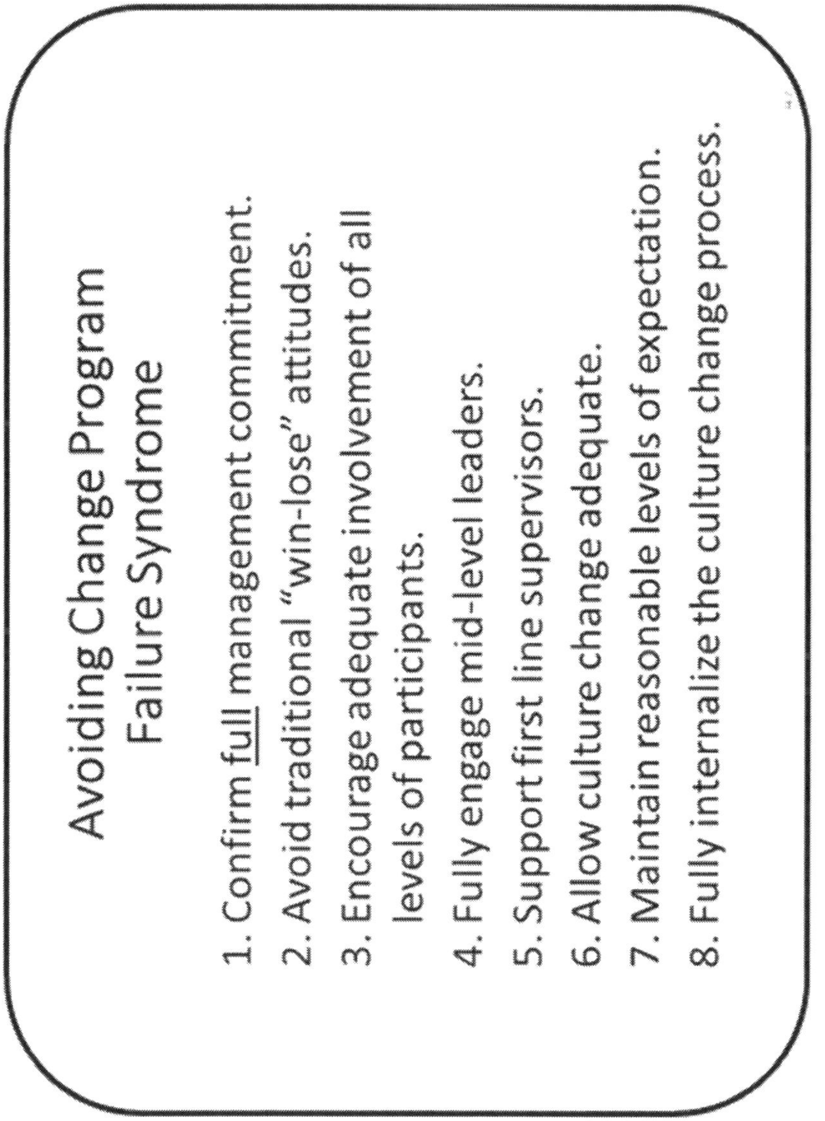

Avoiding Change Program Failure Syndrome

1. Confirm <u>full</u> management commitment.
2. Avoid traditional "win-lose" attitudes.
3. Encourage adequate involvement of all levels of participants.
4. Fully engage mid-level leaders.
5. Support first line supervisors.
6. Allow culture change adequate.
7. Maintain reasonable levels of expectation.
8. Fully internalize the culture change process.

Figure 30

Bob Horton has been active in the environmental field since 1977. He co-founded the Keep Houston Beautiful program first as the Houston Anti-Litter Team and then CLEAN HOUSTON! In 1980, Bob became one of the first recipients of Keep America Beautiful's Professional Leadership Awards. He served for four years on the KAB National Training Team, helping to lead new affiliate project team training workshops in Texas, Oklahoma, New Mexico, and Arizona. In the process, he helped bring dozens of new Texas cities into the KAB fold. While with HALT and Keep Houston Beautiful from 1977 to 1985, he helped pioneer the first U.S. highway adoption programs in America, the Clean Retailer program and the Clean Builder (commercial) program. His Keep Houston Beautiful programs won numerous top awards from Keep Texas Beautiful and Keep Texas Beautiful, some of which are still copied and expanded upon today.

Keep Houston Beautiful was America's first Clean Community System affiliate to serve a population 1,000,000 or more and the first KAB's major city affiliates to win First Place in the challenging National KAB System Awards competition two years back to back.

Made in the USA
Middletown, DE
14 January 2017